MW00881248

To everyone that helped make this book a reality I want to say....

Thank You!

Advanced Praise for *Better OUTCOMES*

"*Better Outcomes* achieves what most leadership books don't— helps those in the middle stages of their career understand how to honestly assess how to become a better outcome driven leader and doing it with purpose and through people. It's practical, insightful, and filled with specific approaches to delivering better results the right way. It should be the go-to for business leaders at any stage of their career—especially as leadership is being re-defined in this more complex business environment."

—**Sandi Peterson**, Partner at CD&R, and former Vice-Chairman of Johnson & Johnson

"*Better Outcomes* is that rare book that has both theory AND practice for how to be successful as a leader. And it is actually fun to read! Steve shows that he is a master at identifying the right things to do and then doing them right. It is now the first book I give anyone seeking to improve themselves and their organization."

—**Stuart McGuigan**, Former CIO of the US State Department, former CIO of Johnson & Johnson, CVS and Liberty Mutual

"Steve distills complex concepts into more relatable, easier to understand, pieces and processes, thus making this an enjoyable read for all levels of experience. His ability to demystify and show the building blocks of success; self-awareness, operational excellence, leadership, and balance gives the reader a simple go-to roadmap to achieve *Better Outcomes.*"

—**Mark Devine**, Head of Data and Analytics, Nike-EMEA

"*Better Outcomes* is superb. It embodies powerful common-sense messages that can help a broad audience. It covers all the steps to success from start to finish and I highly recommend it!"

—**Scott Kline**, Former Group VP, Hewlett-Packard

"*Better Outcomes* is a book that will transform your career…if you are up for the challenge! Steve's mantra of faster-better-cheaper reflects his approach to solving complex business problems across a highly successful career. At his core, Steve is a professor, and this is his lecture on the accountable leadership that is required to drive Better Outcomes for your customers, business, and career. I've been encouraging Steve to write this book for a decade and am thrilled it's finally here!"

–**Mike Reilly**, VP Supply Chain Technology, Johnson & Johnson

"*Better Outcomes* is a must read for anyone looking for a playbook to improve their skills and grow their career. Steve has done an outstanding job of distilling countless years of learning and experience into a concise and practical guide that's full of valuable information and guidance. The advice offered is real, relevant, and engaging. I highly recommend this book to anyone looking to take accountability of themselves, and their career, to the next level."

–**Nigel Storey**, SVP and CTO, Zappos, Amazon

"In a world that continues to accelerate, one can't ignore opportunities to improve personal performance to achieve superior career performance. *Better Outcomes* is one of those rare gifts that provides a simple framework to follow that challenges the reader to think differently to get to their better outcomes faster ever before!"

–**Sasha Koff**, SVP of Digital and Analytics, Dell Corporation

"Based on decades of real-world experiences, Steve weaves his lessons and concepts through *Better Outcomes* into a valuable framework that provides for authentic, outcome-oriented leadership insights that can be quickly applied across any domain or industry."

–**Elinor Riggs**, SVP and Head of Enterprise Programs, Johnson & Johnson Consumer

"I've had the pleasure of knowing Steve for many years and have witnessed much of his professional journey firsthand. *Better Outcomes* reads like a personal journey with him. His writing style blends real world lessons in an easily digestible format with humor and humility. This book will resonate with everyone looking to understand where they are today, how they got there, and what they can do get better outcomes today and in the future."

–**Andrew Simon**, Former Co-Founder and President, Centerline Partners

"*Better Outcomes* does an exceptional job of sharing valuable lessons that Steve acquired during his highly successful career. The insights in this book allow you to learn from someone's experiences and better position yourself for professional success. At the same time, the focus on self-awareness and self-development will better position you for personal happiness in your career journey. This book is an accelerator to leadership learning and leadership success!"

–**Paul Brady**, CIO and Head of Operations, Arbela Insurance

"*Better Outcomes* is right on target, and timely in these complex times. Honest and to the point, Steve distills complex subjects into their basic essences, and thus delivers an easy road map for others to follow, whether they have years, or weeks, of experience."

–**Rocky Silvestri**, Senior Partner, BrightRock Ventures

"*Better Outcomes*… from theory to practice, is what Steve conveys across this book. His simple 'recipes' for success, and breakdown of complex issues into digestible 'bites' makes this an informative and enjoyable read full of valuable lessons for anyone looking to improve themselves, their business, and their career."

–**Carl Debrule,** President, Theron Holdings, LLC

"As someone who has learnt the Dos and Don'ts of leadership, I can personally vouch that every single principle here is field tested! The principles of ASA, doing the right-things-right, and continuous lifelong curiosity & learning, are timeless and available to everyone, if they choose to use them. Read – Digest – Practice the learnings in this book, and I can assure *Better Outcomes* for you and your organization if you make that commitment."

–**Arun Kumar Bhaskara-Baba**, Chief Digital and Information Officer, Honeywell Aerospace

"*Better Outcomes* encourages intense ownership of business outcomes, consistent execution, and fearless leadership. It's a must read for anyone who wants to lead teams and businesses with confidence and courage. Steve's stories and practical advice will help leaders of all levels develop the mental and emotional strength needed to carry their plans forward. A powerful and inspiring read."

-**Christopher M. Smith,** Chief Revenue Officer, Acqua Security

Better
OUTCOMES
They all start, and end, *WITH YOU!*

LESSONS & LEARNINGS FROM A CAREER JOURNEY SPANNING THE MARINES, SILICON VALLEY, AND THE EXECUTIVE BOARD ROOM THAT WILL HELP YOU *ACCELERATE YOURSELF, YOUR BUSINESS, AND YOUR CAREER.*

STEPHEN M. WRENN

Better OUTCOMES

They all start, and end, ***WITH YOU!***

Lessons and learnings from a career journey spanning the Marines, Silicon Valley, and the executive Board Room, which will help you accelerate yourself, your business, and your career!

by Stephen M. Wrenn

Better OUTCOMES Copyright © 2023 Stephen M. Wrenn. All rights reserved. No part of this book may be used or reproduced in any manner without written permission except in the brief quotations embodied in other books, critical articles, or reviews.

Edited and cover by George Verongos

ISBN: 9798375285320

First publication February 2023

Printed in the United States of America

Preface

"It's not about the destination, it's about the journey."

"It's the small things along the way that matter."

"If I only knew then what I know now."

Statements like these, and others that I've heard many times over my career, are just a few of the many reasons I decided to write this book.

I remember hearing these sayings starting in high school and then again and again throughout my career. The people making these statements would also talk about their learning experiences, activities completed, and knowledge they gained that led them to their success.

At that time, I didn't have the experience to truly understand what they were saying. But as my own experiences and learnings progressed, I eventually understood. They were referring to how their own life experiences, which were shaped by what they learned from either doing or observing, influenced their current thinking and capabilities and, in cumulative, made them who they were at that point in time.

The more I heard this narrative over the years, the more I wondered if there was a way to improve upon it. Could the learning curve be shortened so that future individuals and leaders did not have to spend as many years learning things others had learned before? Was there a way to capture this prior learning and trial-and-error experience and then pass it along so others could be more successful faster?

With this thought in mind, I started to keep a journal of my career journey. As I spent time listening, learning, and experiencing things through my journey, I noticed that there seemed to be consistent, repetitive patterns for success and failure across people and businesses. Whether those patterns were around entrepreneurial thinking, spirit, strategy development, financial performance, customer service, sales operations, product quality, etc., they all seemed to coalesce around three key themes: people knowing themselves, people having operational knowledge of how the systems they were in worked, and people understanding the principles and application of leadership.

Now I know this sounds overly simplistic, and in some sense, it is. But that's why I decided to write this book. In a world where things are pretty complicated right now, and getting more complicated every day, there seems to be a need for simplicity and elegance in systems and processes that, when broken down into their essence, are actually quite easy to understand, change, and improve to make our lives easier.

As my career progressed into the executive ranks through the years at different companies, I continued to notice that these patterns stretched across almost all the different businesses and markets I was working in, selling too, or supporting. Regardless of the size of a business in sales or volume, or the location of the business, whether regional or global, it made little difference. (I will state right now that the larger and more multi-national a business or leader becomes, the more complex the problems or opportunities become.) Their business issues or problems were almost always traceable to a loss of focus on the customer, and the three things customers care most about: that the products, services and support they are purchasing are *faster-better-cheaper* for them than ever before.

Over the years, as I worked on solving these issues, I involved many of my industry peers, co-workers, business associates, and friends in lengthy conversations and problem-solving sessions. What I learned in these conversations and sessions was that many of us were trying to solve the same issues or trying to take advantage of the same opportunities, even if we were in totally different places or industries. It was also through these "conversations" that I began to think that just maybe this information would be helpful to others, not just to assist them in solving their problems, but to help them do it earlier and quicker since it became apparent that a lot of our "solves" were through the same trial and error paths.

It was this "thinking" that drove me to write this book because it was very apparent to me that if I had known what signs to look for earlier on my journey, and what potential pitfalls to be on the lookout for, I would have grown my knowledge and capabilities quicker, and contributed more to myself and the places I worked earlier with better outcomes.

In the end, this book is the result of the lessons I have learned across a career spanning many industries, businesses, countries, operational business functions, and universities. One that started many years ago as an air traffic control specialist in the Marines and ended up on the senior leadership teams of multiple Fortune 50 companies, with many stops in between. It is the result of many "what if" moments, endless outcomes analysis, and an understanding of the importance of leadership across it all. I hope you enjoy the book and learn as much from reading it as I did in writing it!

Regards,

Steve

Contents

Preface I

Introduction.. 1

Part I: Better OUTCOMES... *they're about YOU!* 5

Chapter 1: **YOU Today...** *where* and *why?* 7

Chapter 2: **YOU Tomorrow...** *what* and *how?*......................27

Chapter 3: **YOU in the Future...** *ready, set, and almost Go!* .51

Part II: Better OUTCOMES... *they're about Operational Excellence in all that you do!* 65

Chapter 4: **Effectiveness...** *is always 1ˢᵗ!* 67

Chapter 5: **Efficiency...** *doing the Right-Things-Right!* 81

Chapter 6: **Metrics, Targets, and Controls...** *Proving It!* ...109

Chapter 7: **Innovation and Creativity...** *always!* 131

Chapter 8: **The Process of Management...** *science and art!*141

Chapter 9: **The 3Ps... Project, Program, & Portfolio Mgt.**157

Part III: Better OUTCOMES... *they're about applying leadership throughout your journey, start to finish!* 179

Chapter 10: **The Challenge of Leading...** *starts with YOU!*.181

Chapter 11: **The Honor, Understanding, and Challenges of Leading Others...** *leadership applied!* 201

Chapter 12: **Leading Change, Communications, and Time...** *beware the leadership quicksands* 219

Part IV: Better OUTCOMES...*bringing it all together!* 243

Chapter 13: **Continuous Growth...** *through Continuous Learning* 245

Chapter 14: **The Importance of Balance and Resiliency** 257

Chapter 15: **Situational Thinking...** *for Better Outcomes!* .. 269

Acknowledgements 275

Notes • References • Credits 279

About the Author.. 283

Introduction

One thing I wish I'd had when I started down my career path was a how-to guide, one that was useful in explaining a few things along the way. I'm hoping that this book becomes that guide for you. I hope it will help you see things before they happen, help you understand them when they do, and help you respond to them in a way that leads you to a successful outcome. **It is my attempt to simplify and demystify some of the things you may have seen or experienced in your career so far and thus get to a *Better Outcome* faster.**

In *Better OUTCOMES*, I explain patterns and other observations of success I have seen or experienced across the years and break them down into four simple areas with the following focus:

- A focus on having the *right career and business strategy* developed from an in-depth and properly executed opportunity analysis of one's self, one's business, and one's career so far.
- A focus on being more *effective and efficient* by being *faster-better-cheaper* every day.
- A focus on having and *applying leadership characteristics and capabilities* across it all.
- And the importance of having *balance, resiliency, and continuous learning* throughout the journey.

In *Better OUTCOMES*, I try to break down complex terms and examples into simple forms. I use a mix of *applied* knowledge, with many examples drawn from my actual business experiences and *theoretical* knowledge drawn from the prior business writings and research of others. I give credit to these sources in the appendix.

I've tried to include illustrative examples in each chapter that reinforce relativity in business between companies. Regardless of the industry, business is business, and people, their operational execution, and their leadership are more important than anything else. As the book evolves and comes to a close, I will discuss the importance of being a continuous learner, of being balanced in all that you do, and how to remain resilient in the face of adversity across it all.

Part I of this book emphasizes the importance of your self-awareness in getting better outcomes since that is where it all starts. We'll talk about where you are today in your journey and why you are there. We'll discuss why and how to build an *accurate self-assessment* (ASA) of yourself to find your passion and purpose. More importantly, we'll discover what your characteristics and capabilities are, so you can build your own personal journey roadmap. Part I emphasizes the importance of making choices and being completely honest with yourself about your characteristics and capabilities, what you love to do, and what you are good at because you're going to have to live with the choices you make. In the end, it is these choices that drive our happiness and success.

Then we'll move on to methods like a strengths and opportunities analysis and a strategic plan (a real, well-thought-out one) that you can use to better know yourself, what business you are in, why you are in it, what your opportunities really are, and most importantly, to discuss your customers and how to fulfill their needs.

We'll also briefly drop into the basics of good business plans, talking about the importance of having solid financial and implementation plans. Additionally, we'll discuss the importance of the *sales process*, your *quality of product* (QoP) and *quality of service* (QoS), *customer delight,* and the *important role that friends* can play through it all.

Part II discusses the importance of being operationally excellent in all that you do. This thought-provoking, detailed section includes Chapters 4 through 9. It starts with the macro issues of what it means to be effective and efficient and to distance yourself from your competition by doing the *right-things-right*. Part II then dives into the importance of *metrics, targets, and controls* (MTC), why innovation is so important, the *process of management* (POM), and lastly with the 3Ps of *project, program, and portfolio management.*

Part III is about leadership and its importance across your journey, from beginning to end. We will discuss the *skills needed for leadership success*, including characteristics, methods, and approaches. These are the skills you need throughout your career. Unfortunately, these skills take the longest to develop and are too often the least focused on.

Chapters 10 and 11 are about individual *leadership characteristics and the honor of leading others.* We will discuss why it is important to get an accurate leadership assessment of your skills. We will discuss applied leadership and how to be successful doing just that. Then we will investigate what both *servant and situational leadership* are and why they are so important to a leader's success. This part concludes with a chapter on the *importance of change, communication, and time management* to your success as a leader.

Part IV brings everything together in a discussion on *continuous learning, balance, and resiliency.* The section ends with a final chapter providing some ideas on how you can get started today since time's a wasting!

In the end, *Better OUTCOMES* is intended to help you, the reader, think differently. I hope it causes you to question many of the assumptions that have gotten you to where you are today, possibly lay out new or different ones for tomorrow if needed, and gives you the knowledge and incentive to start your journey toward your own better outcomes. I hope that in the end you will be saying, "Wow, I never thought of it that way!" Or better yet, "Now I understand what happened, what is going on and what I can do about it!" And in the end, remembering this…

Sometimes the smallest step in the right direction, regardless of past steps, ends up being the biggest step in your life.

Part I

Better OUTCOMES

… they're about YOU!

Chapter 1

YOU Today
... *where* and *why?*

"If you don't have any idea of where you want to go, or at least a direction, then any road will take you there."

–Joe Gill

So, you have decided to invest some of your time, and money, to embark on this adventure with me, for that I say, "thank you," and I hope you find this book a rewarding journey. One filled with new learning and understanding that ends in you saying, "I'm so glad I read that book, it helped me see and understand things without having to actually experience everything beforehand, and it made me happier and more successful than ever before!"

Now, getting back to this chapter, and more specifically, the quote I use to start it off. This quote is from a very wise person (Joe Gill, a former executive and mentor at Hewlett-Packard) who told me this many years ago and it still sticks with me today. I think of it often, especially when I seem to be going in circles on something, whether it be in my personal or business life, and it always helps me get back on track. How can something so simple be so useful? Well, it is in the essence of what it is saying, that being: *If you don't have an end in mind when you start an endeavor, then how will you know if you are on the right path as you journey down the road?* And more importantly, *how will you know when you "get there?"*

My personal DNA or "fabric" is a scientific or engineering-based persona, "right-brain" oriented as they like to call it, and because of this, I tend to look at things from a "cause and effect" perspective. I identify what caused the effect or outcome to happen, along with the underlying process of the way things work to explain it. Applying this thinking in both my "personal life" and "career life" leads me to think of things as a "journey" with a beginning and end (one day), and thus, the real fun of discovery and learning and hard work is in the middle of this journey.

I call a visual representation of this thinking the *gap analysis model* (shown below). The concept behind it is if you know where you want to go in your personal and/or professional life, and you know where you currently are, then all you need to do is figure out what "actions" you need to take to get there from where you are, or "close the gap." Now, although this may sound easy, I want to stress that it all starts with being able to identify where you want to be in the future (no matter how short or long-term it is from today), which is hard for people to do sometimes. Even harder to do is establish where they are today. These two things form the basis of the thoughts in the following few chapters.

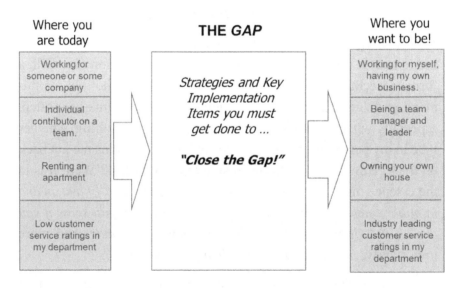

Before we dive into identifying where it is you want to go and where you really are today, one thing I must emphasize is the importance of understanding that even the best of us can't be great at everything we like to do. We sometimes must accept that even though we may not be great at something, we can still enjoy it. An example of this for me is golf. I have decided that it is perfectly fine for me *not* to be great at it, but I still enjoy playing it for the love of being outdoors for four to five hours and occasionally hitting a good shot! The sooner you understand this idea that you don't always have to be great at something to enjoy it, the sooner true happiness will come to you in your everyday activities, but that's getting ahead of ourselves. For right now, let's just start with figuring out where you currently are and how important that is to set up a successful journey.

TODAY... *your current state*

Where am I right now?

"The answer, my friend, is blowing in the wind" are lyrics to an old Bob Dylan song. While they may add up to what is an iconic song, they really are not great words to live by when it comes to your personal life or career direction. Going back to our lead-off chapter quote on direction and destination, spending time figuring out where you currently are in your life is important. When you know where you are, it's the start to understanding if you like it there or if you want to change it. Then you can lay out a plan to facilitate that change so that your future roadmap gets you where you want to go, not where someone else wants you to go or some unplanned road the blowing wind has taken you. This is the cornerstone to the beginning of your change journey. It usually begins with a restlessness of not being happy about where you are today and understanding the reasons behind that "unhappiness" is the key to changing it.

Why am I here, and how did I end up here?

This is one of those questions that is so interesting to ponder and analyze, has so many hidden clues about ourselves, and yet is rarely answered thoughtfully. So, how did you get to where you are today? Was it by accident, by design, by controllable or uncontrollable circumstances, et cetera? Think about it, right now we are all a collective integration of the past, right up to a second ago, a past where we have made decisions consciously and subconsciously that have led us right to this current location and situation. So, my question for you is: "How did this all happen?" What conscious choices did you make, which ones did someone make for you, which ones do you agree with, which ones do you not, which ones can you change (and understand, life's current circumstances mean that sometimes change cannot begin right away as many of you already know), and which ones can you not change? As you can see, there are a lot of things to look at and think about here.

TOMORROW... *your future state*

Where do I want to be, or where should I be?

As I was looking back at my career, one thing that became apparent after a few false starts and wrong or "learning" turns was the importance of clarity of purpose, or the *why* behind the destination I was pursuing. Whether that purpose was to excel in business, become the best version of myself possible, have great friendships, become a "scratch" golfer (ok, not all pursuits get realized, as you may already know), etc., there was always some direction or "thing" I wanted to accomplish. What I realized was that in the parts of my life where I struggled the most, where I didn't seem to be moving forward as quickly or in the direction I wanted, it was almost always because I had either lost focus on the purpose of the outcome I was pursuing, or I had never set or envisioned one to begin with. Without a defined purpose, my direction would waver, my work or daily activities would become muddled, and eventually, my outcomes would be either reduced or, in some cases, non-existent. Think of this as chaos taking over, and eventually, you will end up somewhere, although it may not be where you thought or intended it to be.

Now, as you may have already surmised, sometimes that ending is okay. In fact, occasionally, it may be great, but what I like to say is that luck is a good thing, but eventually, luck will run out, and it will be your focus, your purpose, and your passion which gets you to where you want to be.

So, how did I find my purpose, and how can you? It starts with identifying what gets you out of bed every day. It's about finding what you *love to do* or are *most passionate about doing.* Why is this so important? Because **if you absolutely love what you are doing, and are good at it, then you will never work a day in your life** since it is a pleasure to do whatever you have chosen to do, and while you may be "working" every day, it won't feel like it. For me, that passion and love was, and still is, around working with people to solve business problems.

Warren Buffett, yes that one, knows a thing or two about building a successful career and living a more successful life. In a recent interview for *Inc. Magazine* (Aug. 27, 2022) he gave four tips to consider for your personal and professional growth: ***"do the thing you love, do the things you are good at, learn and practice your good skills, and change the bad ones."*** These are four great tips, ones that very much mirror what I will be expanding on in this chapter and next.

As Warren mentions, along with identifying what you love to do, you need to think about what you are good at, grow those skills, and change or eliminate your "not so good ones." Your final thought being if you can be paid for that love or at least make a living from it, which is a whole other topic.

So, what gets you the most excited to do every day? Is it mountain biking, fishing, reading, helping others, working with animals, growing a business? As you can see, there are lots of things you can be passionate about doing, so now the trick is which one of these, or others, will you choose. To help you figure that out and a few other things about yourself, we start the journey with a process called an *accurate self-assessment* (ASA).

Accurate Self-Assessment (ASA)

While an accurate self-assessment, which is exactly what it says it is, applied to oneself, may sound daunting, it's really a quite simple process. Unfortunately, many people either never think about it early in their career, forget to do it as their career progresses, or only do an ASA when their career performance and outcomes are off track. Over my career, I have seen many managers do or receive an ASA in many ways, but normally it only happens at the yearly review, which is not timely enough or deep enough, to be helpful to anyone.

Just imagine if you were coaching a team and only gave them feedback at the start and end of the game and nothing during— doesn't sound quite right, does it? The ASA is about gathering input about yourself, from yourself and others, which may sound easy, but is actually quite hard because it requires you to be extremely honest with yourself and to encourage extremely honest feedback or input from others to give you the best assessment possible.

Unfortunately, many people, for multiple reasons, are just not open to the gift of feedback and resist hearing what this feedback is saying. This resistance causes them to miss opportunities to stimulate change and growth in themselves. The issue here is that outside perception is "reality," so the input from others is how you are perceived. Whether you agree with it or not, *it is what it is*, as they say, so the sooner you understand that and accept it, the sooner you can get to work on growing or changing when and if necessary.

To get an accurate self-assessment, I have found that the three areas to gather information about are your *characteristics, capabilities,* and *commitment*, what I have labeled the 3Cs.

The 3Cs

In the process of executing an ASA, which will help you better define your purpose through articulating what you love to do and are passionate about, I have found it valuable to go back to the basic elements of myself and see how my DNA is holding up and if it has changed at all. To do that, over the years, I have found that using the following categories, ones that I call the 3Cs, has helped me immensely. I have found that these 3Cs have allowed me, and anyone else, to look at and better understand themselves, which is the first step in moving forward to a different and hopefully better self, career, and outcome.

The Categories of the 3Cs are...

Characteristic: a feature or quality belonging typically to a person, place, or thing serving to identify it. Sometimes used in a statement as "Your defining characteristics."

Capability: the power or ability to do something; the extent of someone's ability. Sometimes used in a statement as "… had an intuitive capability of bringing out the best in others."

Commitment: the state or quality of being dedicated to a cause, activity, etc.; an agreement or pledge to do something now or in the future. Sometimes used in a statement as, "The company or business is committed to quality."

As you can see, these are three easy to understand words, and their definitions generate powerful implications when applied to a person or individual. I am sure many of you in your personal and professional lives have either used them to describe others or others have used them to describe you. Now, let's really dive into them and understand how to use them as the basis for understanding where you want to go, where you should go, and how you are going to get there!

Characteristics

The first of the 3Cs is about you, what makes up your DNA. It's the largest part of any ASA, so it takes time to gather and analyze this information. To do this in the most complete way, it is best not only to self-identify your characteristics but also to have business associates, friends, and family add their input as well. Sometimes this is hard to hear, but it is very beneficial in the long run. You need to be brutally honest with yourself here because, as human beings, we can convince ourselves to believe many good things about ourselves, but is that going to help us get better or get us to where we want to go? Along with getting input or feedback from others, this is also a good time to think about the helpfulness of the plethora of assessment tools available in the industry.

While we are on the topic of assessment tools, here are just a few that I have used in the past that have been very helpful in understanding myself and my characteristics better than I ever could have on my own...

- **360-Degree Feedback**. Most companies have their own version of this assessment tool that is very helpful in getting feedback from coworkers on how they perceive you. Its power is in the process where it gets input from those that work for you, those that work with you, and those that you work for, thus the 360-degree picture.
- **Clifton Strengths Assessment.** From the Gallup organization. Developed by Don Clifton, the father of Strengths Psychology and inventor of Clifton-Strengths, this assessment helps identify your normal personality and breaks it down into thirty-four themes. Over the years, mine have settled on the signature themes of *activator, arranger, responsibility, strategic,* and *woo,* and I have found it very helpful to know I have these themes.
- **Myers-Briggs Type Indicator** (MBTI). This is an introspective self-report questionnaire indicating differing psychological

preferences in how people perceive the world and make decisions. MBTI helps you better understand both your characteristics and also your capabilities, especially your "go-to" preferences. Mine happened to be an ENTJ that over the years migrated to ENTP, and you'll have to do some online research of your own on those to see what they mean. Way too much to cover here, but I encourage you to explore!

- **Korn Ferry's Global Personality Inventory.** This is a tool that assesses your behavior, relationships, and sources of energy/motivation, used for measuring leadership potential in many companies. This is an excellent tool to see if potential new leaders entering your company have the DNA you are looking for.

One quick note regarding these tools—keep in mind that they are all just data points in time, not a defining evaluation of you, so they can and will change over the years (like mine did from ENTJ to ENTP with the Myers-Briggs assessment). So, if you took one or many of them years ago, it would be a good idea to get them done more recently. The results of these assessments should help you better understand yourself, what your potential strengths are, and where you may want to focus going forward.

In doing any ASA, you are going to discover many things about yourself, including traits you currently possess and traits you may choose to adopt. Some of the basic **human characteristics or attributes** that we all have—descriptors like short, tall, eyes, ears, nose, arms, feet, eye color, or hair color—are not the ones that you are looking for or are identified in an ASA. The ones that are not-so-basic attributes and referred to as **business characteristics** are descriptors like: reliable, confident, positive, team player, hard worker, intelligent, good communicator, positive, influencer, et cetera. These are the ones that are usually identified, and the ones you are looking for information on when you do your ASA.

Now, if we take those and then add in what are sometimes described as **leadership characteristics** and/or expectations, we start to see an expanded list about yourself that may look something like this.

- **Trustworthy:** Are you honest/truthful, fair, consistent, dependable, have high-integrity and "walking the talk."
- **Optimist or Pessimist:** Is your glass half full or half empty?
- **Inspiring:** Are you passionate, energized, and engaged?
- **Curious:** Are you open to input from the world?
- **Adaptive and Agile:** How well do you switch gears and remain flexible?
- **Decisive:** How much information do you need for a decision? Do you stand by your convictions?
- **Courageous:** Do you ask for forgiveness or permission to do something new or out of the ordinary? Do you avoid the bumpy road and tough conversations, or do you tackle them head-on?
- **Resilient:** Do you recover quickly from disappoint? Do you learn from your mistakes, adjust, and move on? How do you handle long periods of stressful situations? Are you prepared for them, or do they overwhelm you?

Ok, so you have taken a personal inventory by being brutally honest with yourself on what you see as your characteristics, have gotten feedback from many people on what they think, and have also taken a few assessments to see what they come up with, so you have a personal DNA list. Now it's time to think about how you use your characteristics by turning them into capabilities to be successful.

Think of it this way, you can have all the potential in the world to be successful at something, but if you do not apply that ability, you will never reach your utmost potential.

Capabilities

The second of the 3Cs. These are the things you can do, many times defined by what you have already done. Your characteristics tell you about your fabric, or DNA, as I mentioned. Your capabilities are about the extent of your ability, your "potential" to do things. They are about your qualities, your features, and they are different than your characteristics, which are more ingrained and harder to change. Capabilities are sometimes referred to as skills, but I believe that's an incorrect label since skills really refer to the combination of your characteristics and capabilities being applied—think potential energy compared to kinetic energy. I like to think of it this way, the ability to run is a characteristic that most humans are born with. This capability can then be expanded by learning how to run better, say by joining the track team at your school. Now, if you become a skilled runner, that usually means that you are good at it, fast, or better than average. See the difference?

Keep in mind that you can continually expand your capabilities by learning new ways to see or do things. Still, it's very hard to reduce them since *a mind, once expanded with new knowledge and experience, rarely contracts to its original state.* This is why continuous learning and experiences are so important. Another thing to ponder as you look at your capabilities is this: *do you have twenty years of experience and wisdom, where you expanded your knowledge and capability every year, or do you have one year of experience repeated twenty times, doing the same thing the same way each year?* Only you know the answer to that. Think of it this way: a capability constantly repeated can become a habit, and that can be good or bad—it just depends.

Some other key thoughts to keep in mind as you define and list your capabilities are.

- **What are you educated in? Where is your knowledge focused?** Why did you learn these things? Did you want to go in this direction or were you led into it?

- **What skills do you have and at what level?** You need to be very honest here, saying you are better at something than you are, which is a human tendency, can lead to disappointment in your journey because of a potential career level mismatch. Honesty here will help you set your level so you can get the proper training or education you need to improve or increase your capabilities in an area.

- **Are you an expert in something? What would that be?** This may not be what you do every day, but something you really love to do, and thus have developed a level of knowledge and experience that you don't consciously even think about, but others do.

- **Do you have life experience that differentiates you from others?** This is something many people underestimate and undervalue. Your life experiences make you who you are and tell a lot about you.

- **What do you get passionate or excited about?** Are you good at it? Do you really love it?

- **Are you a problem solver or a problem discoverer?** Don't fret here; the world needs both. People in the engineering or sales field tend to solve problems in front of them, while scientists tend to ponder future problems and look at things from the lens of "what if?" or new possibilities.

- **Are you a coach** (love to see others successful) **or a team player** (want to deeply participate)**?** This helps you decide if you want to move into management or not.

- **Are you good at connecting with others** and influencing them by shaping their thinking?

- **What is your capacity?** Some roles require significant time commitments like long hours, extensive travel, or extended periods away from home and family. There are many roles or jobs that you would love to do, but, due to life's circumstances or timing, would just not work out.

These are some of the things to think about as you build out your list. The more you build out this area—or should I say the deeper you investigate your capabilities and understand the real capability needs of future careers—the better you will understand where your DNA matches up and where you want to apply your capabilities. By understanding your characteristics and capabilities, you develop personal mastery and become an expert in yourself. When you have a clear idea of who you are and what you are capable of, "YOU" starts to become a well-thought-out and internally led force to be reckoned with!

Commitment

The third and final of the 3Cs. Having a sense of commitment is about the action of committing to something. If the career or path you have identified is truly what you love to do, then this part is not that hard because when you love to do something, your commitment to its success will shine through.

What does it mean to be committed or make a commitment? It means dedicating yourself to something like a person, group, or cause. Why is this so important? Because a commitment usually obligates you to do something, and when you commit to something and deliver to that commitment, you establish your trustworthiness. Also, during your career or life journey, you are going to run into challenges, speedbumps, or roadblocks along the way. It is your commitment to your cause, to others, and to yourself that will get you over or through these tough times, period!

The thing about commitment is that it seems to wane over time. Thus, it is easier to make commitments for short-term deliverables, like delivering a monthly report or quarterly project, than it is to deliver on a multi-year plan, so keep that in mind. Also, commitments are made at a certain point in time with a certain level of knowledge. If that knowledge changes, resulting in the need to change a previous commitment, that is okay if you explain that to the person or team you made the commitment to, and they understand why the commitment is being changed. Nothing is more detrimental to one's reputation and career than being known as someone that doesn't deliver on your commitments since that translates into you being perceived as untrustworthy.

Now that you have developed your personal 3Cs through taking assessments, talking to others to get their feedback, and other means, the next step is to analyze them and see what they are telling you. Can you see what your strengths are? What areas do you feel, and does the data say, are your strongest areas? It's important to identify these for yourself because they help you decide what career directions may be best. What about your weaknesses or opportunities for growth? Are they visible to you and data supported? Is it clear to you where you have areas for growth and improvement?

While the 3Cs are very useful in looking inside yourself, one of the hardest things to do is break them down into strengths and weaknesses (or growth areas as some call them). Sometimes these are clear, sometimes they are not. The important thing to understand is that strengths and weaknesses can be situational (dependent upon where you are in life and career) and can change over time. So, it's important at this juncture to spend time on this data and understand how it fits into your current situation. Then see what it means to your future goals and ambitions (we'll talk more about this in the next chapter), and lastly, to make sure you have a solid and truthful picture of yourself as you move forward.

At this time, I find it best to build a small matrix to help see what your strengths and weaknesses are, see which ones you want to grow, and write down your thoughts on these. Here's an example of one that I have used in the past. You can add as many rows and columns as you may need to do your own analysis.

	Strengths	Growth	Thoughts
Characteristics	Trustworthy Optimistic Decisive Courageous	Over-critical Overly data dependent	Learn to make decisions faster
Capabilities	Data specialist	Need global experience	International assignment?
Commitment	What do I want to commit to?	What don't I want to commit to?	Love ESG work

Keep in mind here that although most people love to work on their weaknesses or growth areas first, many assessment advisors recommend, and I do too, that you spend equal time capitalizing on your strengths since understanding and capitalizing on your strengths can give you a big return on your time invested. Yes, shoring up a weakness or two to progress in your life and career is important, but "playing to your strengths," things like optimism and trustworthiness, can be so helpful in situations that they overcome your shortfalls, so do make sure you balance your focus in these two important areas.

The Importance of Identifying Your Future Path

So, you believe you have a good ASA, with all the self-exploration and learning and occasional pain that sometimes comes from doing the 3Cs. You've taken your time to analyze this information, breaking it down into your strengths and weaknesses or growth areas. Now it's time to use this information to help you focus on and choose a path that you can follow for the next few years, one that your passion is derived from, one your skill set is matched to, one that you can and will commit too, and one that you have the courage to implement. So, to help you get started down the correct path, there are just a few more things to think about and identify, which will help you choose your journey's path.

- Do I want to start my own business or work for someone else's?
- What size company would I like to work for or build?

- What are my values and how important are they in choosing a company or industry to work in?
- Where would I like to do it (location, country)?
- What role would I like to do or play?
- What can I do long term, or do I have a defined timeline for my choice?
- What is the result I am looking for; do I have one? Be honest, am I looking for a life-style job, or do I have other ambitions?
- What can I afford to do? Can I make a living at it?

As you can see, each one of these questions opens a new set of questions, and each one will take you down a different path. In the end, all I can say is focus on your passion and strengths and then find industries or roles that require them. You will excel most by maximizing your strengths and minimizing your weaknesses. Roles or careers that utilize your strengths and passions are worth their weight in gold for you!

As we close out this chapter, here are a few things I have always kept in mind along the way, and I think you should too.

First, always remember that:

One of the hardest things to do in life is to leave your comfort zone. But you must let go of the life you're familiar with and take the risk to live the life you dream about.

I have always lived by this, and it has served me well, I think it might serve you well too. Being uncomfortable is how we grow.

Second, luck does happen… and *there is a formula for it!*

There are many things you cannot control, so sometimes it takes a little luck to be successful. Let's face it, who thought surgical masks would be as valuable as they were between 2020 and 2022, or that you could have been a millionaire if you had stock in companies that made hand sanitizer? Go figure.

But real **luck** happens when Opportunity meets Knowledge, Experience, and Preparation.

$$Luck = O + K + E + P$$

Opportunity is always around the corner, sometimes right in front of you, and to seize it or capitalize on it when it arrives, you need to be prepared so you don't miss the opportunity!

Knowledge is the foundation you have built your whole life. All the schools, certificates, books, videos, prior experiences, (if you learned from them) and training you have been consuming your whole life!

Experience, whether it be yours or others, will help you navigate the things that will come up in day-to-day life and dealings. It will allow you to decide which opportunities you should go after and which ones you shouldn't. Experience comes from the breadth, depth, and years of your life's journey.

Preparation is what separates everyone. How well did you prepare today and yesterday for the opportunities today and tomorrow? Do you have the knowledge and experience? How well do you know yourself, your customers, your product or service, your competitors, et cetera? We'll talk more about this in the next chapter. So, are you ready to be lucky?

Lastly, do keep these in mind:

The power of positive thinking cannot be overstated. Having a can-do, glass-half-full attitude will help you through many a tough time, especially in the business world. There are ups and downs to all cycles in life, so keep that in mind. Do not turn simple speed bumps into roadblocks, and do not let anyone else do that to you. If you think you can do it, you can, and if you think you can't, you can't. Which thought do you spend the most time with?

The power of friends is especially important in a time of need and is priceless! I cannot overstate the importance of having a few close friends and advisors available to bounce things off when you have challenges. You need people with no vested interest in your success or failure, just ones who really care about you and want to see you successful and happy!

The power of resiliency, which is the ability to bounce back when dealing with unplanned events, or long times of stress, is paramount to your success (will discuss more in Part IV).

So now that you know what you want to do, why you are doing it, and know you will like it and be successful at it, it is time to head out on the road of "What and How." Well, before we do that, here are a few more thoughts on things to keep in mind to make it a fun trip.

Having a career and a life are not exclusionary, you can have them both, and actually make them into one, which is the best path. You just need to be good at integrating them where needed and partitioning them where needed too. The most successful people have merged them because it is extremely stressful to completely partition them, makes it artificial. So, when you are building your personal journey roadmap, keep this in mind.

The process of building your roadmap is simple. Just think of these four things, two of which you have done already, and our next chapter will explain the other two more clearly.

- Where am I today?
- Where do I want to be in the future and by when?
- How am I going to get there?
- How will I know when I have arrived?

Keep in mind the importance of being flexible, as the future years will be fuzzier and fuzzier the further distant they are. This is okay, just remain flexible and be willing to revise your plan, but it is still important to have some firm stakes in the ground when you start out.

Now it's time to move onto the basics of being successful at what you have chosen to do **by understanding what to do and how to do it!**

To achieve *Better Outcomes*:

- **Today.** Where are YOU and why? How did you get here? Was it by accident or design? Is it where you want to be?
- **Tomorrow.** Where do YOU want to be and why? Do you have an ASA? Do you know your 3Cs? Are you prepared to use them to get to a better outcome?
- **Luck** happens when Knowledge + Experience + Preparation meet Opportunity… are you prepared to be lucky?
- Is your glass half-full or half-empty? The choice of how you see that is all up to you.
- Are your friends helping you believe and achieve, and are you resilient enough to overcome those speedbumps trying to derail you from getting to your destination?

What would you attempt to do if you knew you could not fail?

… think about it.

Chapter 2

YOU Tomorrow
... *what* and *how?*

"Knowing others is wisdom, knowing yourself is enlightenment."

–Lao Tzu

So, you've gotten to the stage of knowing *where* you are today, *why* you are there, *what* you are passionate about, and *where* you want to be in your future. You've identified your own personal strengths and growth areas and have a plan on how to work with them for a successful career. You've thought about and identified different industries, companies, locations, roles, and your values and have made the necessary decisions so that you can be successful in the future. So, with all that behind us, it is now time to dive into *what* to do and *how* to do it!

Over the years of multiple changes down different life paths (because every path has a few detours), I discovered a simple tool that can be used to help you with your personal and professional life's journey. A tool that is easy to remember but not as easy to fill in and stay the course on because it takes discipline and commitment. You can use it to start your journey and then adjust it along the way to keep you on track. This tool is called a SWOT, which is an acronym that stands for *strength, weaknesses, opportunities, threats.*

Your What... *How to start figuring it out*

A SWOT is a strategic process that uses the simple four-quadrant layout tool that I mentioned to help you list and visualize important aspects of yourself and/or your business. It is a process that is taught in many MBA programs around the world, and thus it is used by many businesses annually to set their strategic direction. I have seen companies have varying amounts of success using this process and its visual tool, and what I have noticed is that it's in the execution of the process where the variation in results creeps in.

Why is this? Why doesn't everyone use this simplistic tool to keep them focused and make them more successful? It's in the basic understanding of what is really the content of each quadrant of the tool, how they relate and interrelate to each other, and how they need to be kept simple so they can be acted upon.

The SWOT can be used not only to position a company at the start of its business cycle but also for them to manage that cycle and to make sure that they remain focused on the most important opportunities as the business landscape changes. This also applies when used by individuals for personal growth. Still, again it's the active management of the SWOT that gets neglected for its power.

To better understand what I am talking about here and the power of the SWOT, let's take a deeper look at it.

Basic SWOT Layout

	Strengths	Weaknesses
Internal	What your customer's would say that you do well or better than others.	Issues or problems you have with your business and / or yourself.
External	**Opportunities** Areas for growth in your market, region, client base, etc., not internal improvement areas, those are weaknesses.	**Threats** Think competition, market dynamic changes, and other things that are outside of your control.

| *Leverage* | *Mitigate* |

As you can see from the simple format above, the SWOT layout is easy to visualize and setup, just four simple boxes or quadrants. However, the core of its power is not the setup; it is in understanding that they are four "independent" quadrants that have "interdependency" on each other, and that interdependency use defines the success or failure of its end result.

So where do you start? Well, the first thing is to understand what area of responsibility you are focusing on. What I mean by that is what is the "business unit" you are doing this for? Is it yourself, an independent business owner, where the strengths and weaknesses (S&Ws) may be directly tied to your own ASA; is it for your small business, where the S&Ws are tied to you and your small team; is it for a business you are brand new in or starting up; is it for the division or area you are managing in a larger company where the S&Ws are about your whole area of responsibility? These questions are very important to answer right up front because it helps you identify your customers and competitors that you form your questions around. Now let's dive in!

Strengths and Weaknesses:

These two quadrants are what I call your "internal truths," which are the things that you can control, are absolutely true (direct input from customers, friends, and other primary data), and you can focus on to either leverage or change.

S is for Strengths

What are you, your business, or your corporate business area of responsibility good at? What can you do that can be used to differentiate you and your business from others; what can you do that is different than all others and can be sustained? Don't short yourself here—having outstanding resiliency is a differentiator in many businesses and in life in general. If you are truly good at that, and others would say so, then write it down. Where are you faster, better, or cheaper (think higher value) than your competitors and why? Remember, perception is reality, so unless your "customers" would say or agree with what you are thinking or saying here, it is not real, and the inverse is true; if they say it, but you don't agree with it, then they win! Same if you are doing a personal SWOT; this is where input from your co-workers, friends, family, etc., becomes very valuable.

What are the pitfalls? Well, that's in you not being as honest or detailed enough with your input here. I hate to say it, but everyone loves to claim they have great people working with or for them or are on a great team, but is that enough to differentiate you from others, or is it the price for just being in the game, as they say? Something like long-term team stability that allows your team to function faster and better than your competitors or deliver customer service that others can't because of customer knowledge or depth would be great ones, but just putting down *great team* or *great employees* won't be sufficient. I wish I had a nickel for every time I heard someone say this; I'd be very rich by now!

When you are thinking about putting down a certain strength, ask yourself if it is better than average or just average. Your answer to this question will be extremely helpful in making sure you have strengths listed that you can use as a competitive advantage later, so be as honest and data-driven as you can here.

W is for Weaknesses

What do you wish you, your business, or your corporate business area of responsibility could do better? What products are you missing? What would your customers say they would like to see you do better or where are you not serving them and why? Slow order fulfillment or customer service—those are weaknesses. High prices or manufacturing costs—those are weaknesses. High employee turnover—a definite weakness. This is an area that is easy to collect data on, especially in today's social media-based world. The real challenge is culling the sometimes-overwhelming feedback into the core of your weaknesses. What's causing that slow customer service? Are there not enough customer service people? This could also be causing the high turnover, which is why analysis of your weaknesses and getting to their root cause is very important to fixing them. Solving the problems you know you have is usually never the issue, solving the right problems is. This is an area where having some formal training in problem-solving (yes, there are many courses on how to do this well, Kepner-Tregoe is a good one I have used in the past) can give you a large return on your investment quickly since solving the wrong problems can be very costly in time and money.

In this quadrant, strength can become a weakness, especially if this is a personal SWOT, if you have too much on it, use it too much, or it's not applied correctly. This is sometimes hard to identify. Being seen as having a "high customer touch" can be great sometimes, but in others it just may be too much. Think of how many times you get customer feedback or service requests after a company does something for you; it can be a little overwhelming sometimes, can't it? *Too much of anything is usually not good*, and thus a strength can become a weakness if over-applied.

One last thing to keep in mind on this topic, human beings tend to be overcritical of themselves, especially entrepreneurs, so keeping this quadrant to just the top five weaknesses can sometimes be daunting. Make sure you prioritize your list, no matter how long it gets, to the five most important weaknesses; that's going to be your biggest challenge here. If you don't do that, then you will have the issue of spreading your scarce resources too thin to solve the issues at hand, like I mentioned earlier. Better to solve one and then move on to the next one and add more later than to spread everyone too thin, and thus nothing gets solved, or nothing gets solved quickly.

Opportunities and Threats:

These are your *external truths*, the things that are going on in your markets or industry. The things that can help or hurt you and your business that you can't control but you can leverage/capitalize on to take advantage of or be prepared to avoid or minimize the impact of.

O is for Opportunities

After identifying your strengths and weaknesses, it is now time to turn your attention outward and identify what the opportunities are in the marketplace, industry, business, or yourself that can be capitalized or improved upon.

One thing to quickly remember here is that if this is your own "personal" SWOT, then the opportunities are "internal" to you. They are the things you have identified about yourself that you want to improve on. They are like weaknesses but different because these are mainly new "opportunities" for you, not areas that you already do or behaviors you already have that you want to improve; these are things you want to add to be better, or maybe just different. Some examples would be becoming a writer, taking up cooking, or learning how to fly, these could all be new hobbies, or you could think of them as steppingstones to new careers. The choice is yours. The items in your personal opportunities section are all things you can do to grow that you haven't done already.

Now, getting back to looking at opportunities for your business or company, the thing to remember is that data is very much your friend in this quadrant. This is where you need to look at a lot of those "pre-SWOT" questions we listed earlier, like size of the market, which direction is it moving, who your competitors are, et cetera. It is good to expand your end horizon here and think in terms of what your opportunities will look like twelve, eighteen, and twenty-four months from now, not just in the upcoming year. This is the quadrant where creativity and innovation kick in. I try to hold on those because they are usually the solves for the opportunities you see, but many times get put in here, and thus the solve becomes the focus rather than the reason for the solve, which is what should be here. Listing a new product being launched or a service being offered is not the opportunity; listing why you came up with these products or services to begin with is. You may have heard people in the industry or leadership refer to things as "that's an engineering-driven product" or "that product or service is a hammer looking for a nail." These are all examples of things that were developed without a clear opportunity identified, and thus, many times, they are never as successful as they could have been or outright failures because no one ever understood what problem they were solving (the opportunity).

When I think about something I wish I had known when I was starting out, it is the importance of using high-quality timely data in this quadrant and not just past experiences to define your opportunities from the outside in. Whether it is industry-provided benchmarking data from companies like Gartner or Forester, company annual reports, S&P 500 analysis, etc., it's always crucial to have current and thorough data in this quadrant, along with your experience, so that you can make good decisions around what to do next. You must be able to understand the difference between a customer want and need, what is a trend or just a fad, what is short-term or long-term, and in the end, how to integrate all this information together so you can make some choices. So, the more you use real data to identify, frame, and highlight the opportunity, the better the result of this step will be. Not to undervalue people's experience and prior learnings in this quadrant, they are still very valuable. But with the advent of things like machine learning (ML), artificial intelligence (AI), and predictive analytics in the last few years, opportunity identification is now less about the long-term experiences of others (since many of those are not based on current technology of business capabilities) and more on being able to predict what may happen going forward in this new world order. Scary and exhilarating stuff here.

One caveat I like to add, as I mentioned previously, is that luck does get involved occasionally, so even if you don't have supporting data, you can drive to success. I always like to point out that many times while we are searching for a solution to an opportunity we see, we come up with something that we may not have been looking for. Duct tape and Post-it Notes are both great examples of products that were "discovered" while people or companies were looking for something else. Who could have predicted the success of the iPad, which got introduced exactly at the right moment in time, when the networks were just moving from copper to fiber transmission lines, allowing all that rich video content to become available on a screen in your hands. Let's face it, sometimes, it's good to be lucky!

Now, the opposite of this would be the small business entrepreneurs that open because it is their passion and not because of deep research through data. Things like a coffee shop, bakery, clothing store, etc., and other types of small businesses fail at a rate of greater than 90%, with much of that due to poor initial data analysis and research. So many small business failures could have been avoided with the proper due diligence on the opportunity in this section, spending the time to scope the market and the business opportunity before going after it.

This brings me to my last point on this very important quadrant, the term **faster-better-cheaper**, a litmus test I have used for all my opportunities and ideas for over thirty years, and one I still find very relevant today.

I will expand on this term in-depth in the next chapter, but right now, I want you to understand the importance of asking yourself questions around these three attributes. If your idea will give your paying customer something *faster* than before or *better* (higher quality) and, at the same time, they perceive it to be *cheaper*, which means it has a higher value or lower cost for it, then you will end up with a **delighted customer**. The opportunities that hit all three of these customer wants/needs are the ones you should spend your time and money on right away!

T is for Threats

Think external and big picture first. Is the market for your product and or service slowing down? What macroeconomic factors are affecting your industry that you must be concerned about and address? Think about it: how many companies can you name, without trying too hard, that missed their opportunities because they didn't take the threats seriously enough? I think about technology company names that are no longer around because somehow they missed the external threat to their products that others saw. For instance, the Wang Corporation had the original word processor but missed that everyone needed one, not just businesses, so they missed the external threat of competitive new market entries. Digital Equipment (DEC) and SUN Microsystems had proprietary software operating systems and missed the move to standard operating systems, which is where Microsoft went. And products like the Palm Pilot and Blackberry both missed the warning signs of the importance of open applications. Threats is the area where you must think about actions that may "cannibalize" your own products or services. Better you do that to yourself before someone else does it to you. Tough decisions need to be made here.

The biggest thing to think about when listing threats to yourself or your company is to think macro first, taking into consideration all markets and industries, and then micro forces, like the new products and services of your industry and competition. The tendency in the threat quadrant is *not* to think both broadly and deeply. List only what we can see, not what may be coming down the road. This quadrant lends itself well to a thought session with your team where you bring up "what-ifs" around your competition, your industry, and other things going on in the outside world.

One last note, SWOTs sometimes get ignored after they are done because of our tendency to list too many things in each section. Ask yourself if you are focused on the critical few or the trivial many? My recommendation from experience is that you hold each section to five points or fewer. This is not a more-is-better situation. In fact, having too many things to go after causes a "defocusing" or "spreading" of scarce resources, which is one of the main reasons many corporate and personal growth and improvement initiatives fail.

Quadrant Inter-Dynamics

Now that we have all the quadrants filled in, the next thing to understand is how they interact with each other, the interdependency that I mentioned earlier. Take a look at the updated diagram here. See the arrows that have been added in? They are there to remind you that these four quadrants have dependencies on each other that you should keep in mind and use to your advantage when possible. Now, let's discuss those some more.

Basic SWOT showing Quadrant Inter-Dynamics

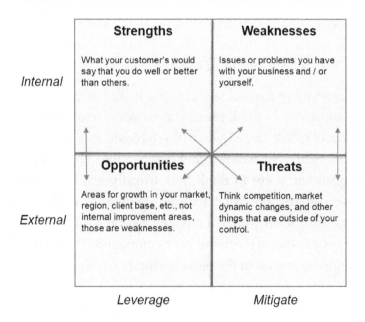

	Strengths	**Weaknesses**
Internal	What your customer's would say that you do well or better than others.	Issues or problems you have with your business and / or yourself.
	Opportunities	**Threats**
External	Areas for growth in your market, region, client base, etc., not internal improvement areas, those are weaknesses.	Think competition, market dynamic changes, and other things that are outside of your control.
	Leverage	*Mitigate*

Cross Arrows: They tell you that there is a relationship between strengths and threats and between opportunities and weaknesses. This means you may be able to use your strengths to offset any imminent threats and see if any weaknesses may prevent you from taking advantage of an opportunity. If there are weaknesses that could impact your taking advantage of an opportunity, then you will need to address them BEFORE you go after the opportunity, or you will risk having the weakness interfere with it.

Vertical Arrows: These tell you to look at your strengths to see if they can help you immediately move on an opportunity. Then look at your weaknesses and see if any of the threats may be accelerated because of them (your competitors are constantly looking for these in you). Think of it this way, if you have a hole in your boat (weakness) and there is a big storm coming (threat), you might want to get all resources focused on that hole before it is too late and sinks you!

So, as I mentioned at the beginning of this section on SWOTs, you can see it is not complicated, but it is the discipline to do it right from the beginning and then to review and update on a continuous basis. That is how to make sure your SWOT is as powerful as it can be.

Now that your SWOT and ASA are done, it's time to pull all that wonderful information into a solid plan, which starts with establishing a strategic direction.

Strategic Direction… *finalizing your What*

Now you have a better understanding of yourself and your capabilities, know your strengths, weaknesses, opportunities, and threats, and have identified areas you would like to expand and grow. It's time to pull that all together with a few more things—like your core values, guiding principles, and ethical grounding—to build your strategic direction.

The basic definition of a strategy is the application of strengths against weaknesses and/or strengths taking advantage of opportunities… sounds familiar, right? The essence of a great strategy is starting with a firm knowledge of yourself and what you are trying to accomplish, but there are still a few things missing. Back when you did your ASA, your analysis was mainly about you in an external sense (what you do, what you like to do, how the world perceives you, et cetera). It didn't ask questions about what your values are, what you believe in, or what your guiding principles in life are. While some of that may have come out when you discovered what you were passionate about or what type of companies you wanted to work for, much of it was not addressed. This is the time to do that.

Your strategic direction is forged in you—who you are, what you are passionate about, what your capabilities are, and what you stand for. In this final step, before getting into action plans, it is up to you to identify what you stand for (or against) and decide how that is going to influence or affect your career going forward. Only you can answer that, and it is a question, or questions, I recommend that you do before moving on to your strategic plan. Your strategic direction is constantly calculated by referring to your moral compass, core values, and your "North Stars" (the things that ground you), and it's the glue that holds everything together when the going gets rough. It's what you come back to time and time again to make sure you are on the right road, and without a well-done strategic direction based on your moral compass, things will tend to constantly drift, and success will be elusive. Try your hardest to identify what values and morals you live by (or want to live by) and try your hardest to get them aligned in both your personal and professional life. You'll be grateful you did and more successful too!

The How... *making it into a reality, the Strategic Plan*

So, you have identified your strategic direction, now it is time to take that and **build a comprehensive strategic plan.** A strategic plan is where you bring together your SWOT and strategic direction and add more details around the measurable goals and objectives you are trying to achieve, along with time-based implementation steps you are going to use to achieve them (think back to GAP diagram). Did all your hard work collecting and analyzing data and formulating your strategic direction point you to *doing the right things?* The ones that you feel will help you get to where you want to go? If you have been honest and truthful to yourself, then I'm sure the answer will be yes to this, and thus now it's time to expand on the details for implementation.

The Strategic Plan

A strategic plan is a document stating the direction you want to go in, the measurable goals you want to achieve, and implementation plans and action items you must execute on to get there. Think of it as the complete story and plan for your trip, which you then execute, measure, evaluate, and adjust against. It should then be kept up to date to track progress and analyze where you may need to adjust so you are still arriving at your end target as planned. Why is a strategic plan so important? Because a strategic direction is not a plan. The actual strategies are not detailed enough to hold people accountable yet, thus you need some more "meat on the bones" to define your different strategies. Also, what you decide to leave out of your strategic plan is as important as what you choose to include in it, so keep that in mind.

- **Business Strategic Plan:** The *whats, whys,* and *hows* at a high level of what you are looking to achieve in your business. These are what you plan to focus on, **derived from your SWOT opportunities.** It is a good idea to put your SWOT matrix in this section of your strategic plan, so you have it as a reference as your timeline or year progresses. This should be some of the specifics on how you are going to go after those opportunities, with details on the following.
  o Industry and market trends
  o Competitive analysis (what are they doing and why, what do you think they will do?)
  o Opportunities expanded upon
  o Measurable goals and objectives

Think about how you are going to go after the opportunities you identified, what your timing is, what resources you will need, and what information you will need on an ongoing basis to keep on track. What are you going to deliver to yourself or the corporation if you successfully complete all your objectives? Is it where you wanted to go, or should it be?

Think of this as a section you can pull out to explain all the rest of the pieces at the highest level. The one that you can share with your boss, your banker, or your board of directors to best describe the *whats, whys,* and some of the *hows,* and how they are all connected. Questions for you in this section should include:

o *Am I being bold enough or too conservative?* (Hitting every goal all the time usually points to being too conservative. If you are being bold and stretching yourself, you will occasionally miss goals, but that's okay; the learning from that is worth the miss.)

o *Are my goals and objectives (G&Os) easy to understand and are they energizing to rally around, or do they always need someone to explain them and get people excited?* Believe it or not, the easier things are to achieve, the less people get excited about them; people like reasonable stretch goals and objectives that challenge them.

• **Product Strategic Plan:** The *whats, whys,* and *hows* for your product. You mention these things in your business plan, but they are detailed here for each product and its direction. While you need all the standard information here, roadmaps around product positioning within your product lines and against competitor ones, you also need to discuss pricing strategies, promotional strategies, and distribution strategies.

I could dive deeper into each of these areas, and doing a sub-strategy for each one is recommended, but I am going to leave that for you to look at on your own because there is too much to cover on each of these topics to do them justice here at this time. I do recommend you look at some of these topics in other books, like Michael Porter's *Competitive Strategy* comes to mind as a good place to start.

Getting back to questions you should be asking yourself in this section, besides the topics I mentioned above, they resemble something like these.

o *What aspect of my product or service am I differentiating myself with?* Is it product features, product pricing, or product quality, or am I competing on a service strategy like faster delivery, easier-to-use order process, better customer "touching," and responsive team? If it is the second answer, then you need to include this information in your service strategic plan.

o *How am I positioned against my competitors in performance, price, and overall value?*

o *Is my pricing competitive?* If not, do I have sound reasoning that explains the difference to my customers?

- **Service Strategic Plan:** The *whats, whys,* and *hows* for your services and your positioning of them. This could be part of your product strategic plan if the purpose of your services is just to support them so that you sell more of them, or it could be a totally separate plan if your purpose is to build a separate business around your services. The thing about a service strategic plan is that no matter which way you decide to position your services (and you can do it both ways at the same time, which is how car dealers and other types of businesses do it), just make sure you detail it out, not just handle it as an add on to your product strategy. Service strategy needs to be defined, understood, and then driven back into your operational processes so that everyone understands the high-quality functioning specifications of your products and the commitments made or guaranteed around things like on-time delivery, locations of delivery, et cetera.

In the end, your service strategic plans are about meeting the commitments you have made to your customers or should have made, around having *the right products and services, in the right place, at the right time, with the guaranteed level of quality you committed to.*

- **People/HR Strategic Plan:** Now that you have your business, product, and service strategic plans done, it's time to put deep thought into the resources you need to get the work done. While resources mean many things, like materials to build products, buildings to house inventory, inventory itself, and money to fund projects, the most important resource to any company's success are its human resources. Which is why companies have HR departments to begin with.

So, when thinking about your human resources, here are some questions you should start asking about what is needed to support the plans you have put together.

o *What are the types of expertise or roles needed, and how many of each type do I need to get the work done?*

You should work with your current leaders to do a work hour analysis and understand how many hours it takes to get the work done, which is not an easy thing to do. Lots of variables come into play here that make work longer than it should take; things like waiting for signatures, waiting for people on vacation, too many meetings, etc., are productivity killers. Hire what you need to do the work, not to run possible inefficient processes or procedures inside your company.

o *Where do I need the people located? Do they need to be close to the customer or close to the work, or maybe even close to each other?*

As you can see, COVID made everyone have to rethink this plan. Telecommuting and remote work is now more accepted than before, which I believe is a good thing.

o *Do they need to be full-time or part-time? Can they be contractors, or do I need full-time employees?*

Here you should be thinking about how long the work is going to take, whether it's ongoing or project-based; is it something you want and have to do forever, or does it have a defined end date? Nothing is worse and more impactful to an individual than getting laid off, so making sure you need a full-time employee on the team is one of the most important things you can do. It's always better to have someone come on as part-time or a contractor for a while than to immediately hire for full-time. This way, you can see for sure if you need the role or new capacity and avoid the bad practice of hiring and firing, which is not a good thing, yet companies continuously have to learn this again and again.

o *Have I taken things like employee turnover and certain role shortages in the industry into consideration?*

This is an area that became very impactful during the pandemic and afterward, when unemployment dropped to 3% levels and thus created an extreme worker shortage. This shortage caused many businesses to have to alter their strategic growth and/or service plans because they could not find the workers to deliver the plans, which reinforces why having an HR plan is so important.

o *Do I have well-defined diversity, equity, and inclusion plans? Are they measurable? How will we know if we are making progress in this extremely important area?*

This is an extremely important area for the success of any HR plan and overall company strategy. Having a diversity of thought is so important to making well-thought-out decisions that have many different points of view. The term "group think" has been applied to many decisions that have not turned out the way companies or leaders have wanted, which is often due to not having diversity of thought. As most statisticians know, the more diverse that data population is in a set of data being analyzed, the better the analysis will be. What leaders are finding out now is very much the same thing, the more diverse the team is that is making decisions, the better those decisions will be.

o *Do I have defined training plans for myself and my employees so that we can grow our capabilities as we progress as a company and team?*

Don't forget the importance of both technical and soft-skills training. The latter always seems to get missed in the business world, and I would argue that it is many times more important than the technical skills. Sometimes a small improvement in things like teamwork training gives a bigger return than more technical training because a whole team working better together is more impactful to the outcome than just one person being better.

- **Financial Strategy/Plan:** Why do I wait and do this after the first three strategies because if you do this first, then you tend not to be as honest right up front about what you really need to make things happen. You will always need to adjust to the $$$ you have, but best to do this last so that you can see what is required to execute the plan before you make decisions on what to fund and what not to.

In the financial area, there are a couple of simple equations you should always keep in mind, whether you are running your own business of one or leading a group of thousands.

Income = Revenues – Expenses, which is pretty much the same way you handle your checkbook or online accounts in your personal life. The *cost of goods sold,* **COGS = Labor + Materials + Overhead**, which is about the true cost of producing something. Understanding these two equations and their relationship to your business operations, along with a few things about taxes and depreciation, and you are well along the path to running and leading a profitable business.

A few more financial things to keep in mind.

- o **Revenue thoughts...** What is selling? What isn't? Do I have the right pricing? How do I know?

- o **Expense thoughts...** What does each product or service cost me to produce and deliver? Do I have the delivery details that include logistics like storage and shipment and returns by each individual product/service? Am I doing activity-based costing or just averaging everything together?

- o **Income thoughts...** Do I have my gross income (sometimes referred to as gross margin or GM) by product or service, so I know what my most and least profitable products and services are? This is extremely important. As businesses grow, they often lose sight of this and are selling some products they are actually losing money on because the price of the product has dropped below what it costs to build and deliver it.

- o **Competitor thoughts...** Do I know what my competitors charge for similar products/services? Do I know how my products and service levels compare to theirs?

So, as you can see, there are many questions to ask and answer, and these are just the tip of the iceberg. Whether starting your own business, or as an employee of a larger business, I recommend that you obtain and/or refresh some basic education on all the financial aspects of your business. The return on your time investment can be huge!

Moving on to Implementation Plans

Each of these five plans needs an implementation plan, and more importantly, they need to be connected and integrated as part of the overall strategic plan. Still, they are to be drawn from each individual area. Looking at the following strategic plan diagram, see how it has arrows added? See how these arrows are all connected? This shows you why it must all be one integrated or connected implementation plan for the best outcome. This is what the outcome should be, but it rarely is, and it becomes especially difficult as companies grow, and company "silos" begin to develop.

How often have you seen plans done in separate functional areas that have conflicting G&Os that work against each other rather than with each other? So, how do you keep your plans from working against each other? Well, one way is to use a simple four-step process that I have used over the years. I call it EMEA, which stands for *execute, measure, evaluate, and adjust.* It is a simple yet powerful way to keep each of your plans connected and your outcomes on target.

- **Execute:** This is where implementation plans, action plans, monthly plans, and quarterly plans are all acted upon. It is about activities that deliver on your roadmap to move you toward your destination. Things like goals, objectives, initiatives, and measures of success are all spelled out with a visible plan to do them. If done correctly, you should be able to trace it all back to your gap analysis that we discussed in Chapter 1. It should answer the main questions in the gap, spelling out how you are going to close the gap!

- **Measure:** The most important step in this process, it is the one that makes sure you are successful end-to-end in your plans by making you stop and think about what you are measuring. What I mean by this is that the success of any strategy and its execution is not how many measures or *key performance indicators* (KPIs) you have; it's about having the right ones, ones that people share, ones that complement each other, ones that connect each department, ones that your people can understand and use to drive their performance and outcomes every day. I will expand more on how to do this in Chapter 6. What I will leave you with here is to remember that more is less in this area. When looking at your measures, think about what the absolute minimum is that you need to keep everything moving along, not every little thing you want to see.

- **Evaluate:** the importance of true evaluation from actionable data from your measurements cannot be overstated. You are not evaluating to look good or get a nice report card; you are evaluating, so you know where and why to adjust. As I mention in the preceding **measure** section, we like to use measures as a report card to say we are doing a good job rather than as a story tool to show us where we have opportunities to be better, showing us where we have **not** done well, which is hard for most people to admit. The way we should look at performance indicators or measures is not that we met our target—let's say more than 95% customer satisfaction—but what is the 5% telling us about where we didn't meet the target? This is where the true improvement information lies.

A good example of how the power of thought can impact your measurement and evaluation processes is in a study done by the University of Michigan back in 1982. At that time, Japanese automobile companies, mainly Toyota, were doing so well, and the top three US car makers were losing market share fast. During this study, they discovered one of the major differences was their approaches to reporting and data. It was discovered that US car makers looked at data and used it to show how well they were doing, especially liking to use green, yellow, and red to show their performance against their targets, very much like a report card. While Japanese car makers (Toyota) looked at data in the opposite direction. Where they had not achieved 100% of an outcome, they tried to figure out why they had any defects at all; two very different approaches indeed, resulting in a very different outcome.

- **Adjust:** Okay, so your "system" has shown you where you have opportunities to be better; now what? How you approach this area is critical to its success. You need to be focused, deliberate, and inclusive here, not jump around every time you see a piece of data or measure that is RED or not moving in the right way. Although speed is a good thing here, too much speed is just reckless. You need to understand why your original plans did not work correctly before you try to get a different outcome. Again, a good way to think of your "adjustment" is as if you are on a journey, flying from New York to San Francisco. As you know, there are many variables that can interrupt that journey, things like mechanical problems, weather, strikes, et cetera. Each one of these has a different solve, but the most important thing is that you adjust according to the event. The earlier, the better because it's the last-minute adjustments that cause the most stress and cost the most, as many of you can probably attest.

So, what have I learned over the years to make sure I have developed a good strategy? Here are some questions I ask myself

- Is my strategy simple and focused?
- Does it deal with real issues or opportunities that will grow me or my business, or does it avoid the "elephants in the room?"
- Does my strategy cover all parts of my business?
- How does it compare to my competition?
- Can it be acted upon and measured?

Let's wrap this chapter up. Remember, a long list of strategies or objectives is not a strategic plan. It is simply a long list of things to do that will keep you and everyone else busy, but maybe not on the right or most important things. Keep focused, know what you must do, make sure you are *doing the right things*, make sure those *things* are connected to something that is better-faster-cheaper for the customer, get it done, then repeat on the next most important thing or strategy!

To achieve *Better Outcomes:*

- **YOU Tomorrow…** do you know what you want to be or where you are going?
- Are you going after your defined opportunities? Are you adjusting to take advantage of opportunities as they present themselves, or are you rigid and inflexible?
- Are you addressing your weaknesses so that they don't inhibit you from taking advantage of your opportunities?
- Have you defined your strategic direction, so you know whether you are on the right path or not?
- Do you have a strategic plan, with all the parts and details?
- Are you executing, measuring, evaluating, and then adjusting (EMEA) today for tomorrow?

Ultimately, effectiveness and growth are about making good choices, doing the right things, and not trying to do everything.

… think about it.

Chapter 3

YOU in the Future
... ready, set, and almost Go!

*"It's far better to dare mighty things, to win glorious triumphs,
even though checkered by failure, then to take rank with those
poor spirits who neither enjoy much nor suffer much, because
they live in the gray twilight that knows not victory, nor defeat."*

–Theodore Roosevelt, 1899

Ok, so far, you are moving nicely along a checklist in your quest to move forward better and faster in yourself and your career. In Chapters 1 and 2, you noticeably accomplished the following.

- Understand where YOU currently are...   check √
- Understand how YOU got there...   check √
- ASA completed and you know what YOU are good at...check √
- Know what YOU love and are passionate about...   check √
- Have defined where YOU want to be in the future...   check √
- Have an idea on what YOU need to do to get there...   check √
- Have made the commitment to go forward and have the intestinal fortitude to stay the course during the difficult times that will be encountered on the journey.........double check! √√

So, you have made some tough decisions because you have been brutally and completely honest about your characteristics, capabilities, commitment, and courage, right? Because you are now going to move from planning into your implementation stage of the journey. If you haven't been honest, then you may either end up at the wrong destination, or your journey may be much more difficult than it needs to be.

It's time to get going, right? Well, the answer to that is yes and no. Before we get going, I need to mention some things about the importance of quality, customer service, the sales process, and teammates and friends that hopefully will contribute to a more pleasant and rewarding journey.

The Importance of Quality in all That You Do

Quality of your deliverable, whether it be you as a single person LLC or as part of a Fortune 50 conglomerate, is always about quality in the eyes of your customer (both internal and external). This is where "the rubber meets the road," as they say. In today's "digital" world, a customer's bad quality experience can spell the difference between success or failure in a nano-second. We have seen the speed by which a bad review will hit the internet in today's social media world. Look at the following graph. It tells you all you need to know about the importance of great customer service and the impact it can have when it isn't there.

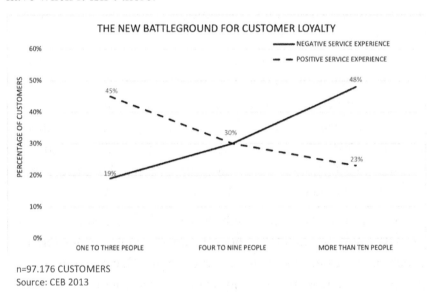

THE NEW BATTLEGROUND FOR CUSTOMER LOYALTY

n=97.176 CUSTOMERS
Source: CEB 2013

As you can see, a negative customer experience will reach many more people than a positive one will, so let's keep that in mind and remember good enough is only good enough if the customer agrees.

Almost all customers can agree that they are constantly looking for products and/or services to be faster-better-cheaper all the time. It is the competitive differentiator that they feel. In the past, it was thought and proven that although customers wanted all three of these things all the time, they could rarely get more than two at a time. Why was that? Because if they got it better and faster, then it costs more. If they wanted it cheaper and faster, it didn't have the quality or features they expected. And many times, if they wanted it better and cheaper, then it took too long to get. Not so today, with the advent of newer technologies, better access to data, social connections, and sourcing. It is now more possible than ever to make sure you can and do deliver faster-better-cheaper all the time (and that cheaper can be higher value, as I mentioned before). Because if you don't do it, someone else will, and your customers will migrate to them. It's only a matter of time.

So, how do you make sure you are delivering a high-quality experience all the time? That's through the process we call **quality assurance** (QA), simply defined as the maintenance of a desired level of quality in a product or service by means of attention to every stage of the process of delivery or production. Which is really the combination of quality planning, quality engineering, and quality control, the definitions of which are:

- **Quality Planning** (QP): Document(s) that specify quality standards, practices, resources, specifications, and the sequence of activities relevant to a particular product, service, project, or contract.

- **Quality Engineering** (QE): A discipline of engineering concerned with the principles and practices of products and services to deliver quality assurance. Focuses on making sure that goods and services are designed, developed, and made to meet or exceed customers' expectations and commitments.

- **Quality Control** (QC): The set of measures and procedures to follow to ensure the quality of a product or service is maintained and improved against a set of benchmarks. Any errors that are encountered are either eliminated or reduced. The focus of this action is to ensure that the outcomes meet the product or service specifications and commitments.

With these three areas in mind, QP, QE, and QC, you now apply the thinking that everything, especially in the business world, can be looked at, and in most cases treated, as a process with a cause and effect. The essence of *assuring* you deliver a quality product and/or service to your customer is nothing more than planning for it, engineering the capability to do it (these are the *causes*), and then putting in the controls to measure the *effects* of your causes, thus allowing you to prove to all that your plans are being delivered and your *guarantees* are being met.

Before I close this area out, I'd be remiss if I didn't mention some of the more important quality management and control tools here, some of which are:

- **Cause and Effect Diagram:** Used to brainstorm and explore all possibilities. Also referred to as a fishbone or Ishikawa diagram.
- **Check or Observation Sheet:** Helpful in seeing what is really going on (don't tell me, show me). Pilots use this, it's called their pre-flight checklist, that's why they walk around their plane before they get in, visible inspection against checklist.
- **Process and Value-Stream Maps:** Used to understand interdependencies (picture is worth a thousand words) and make processes visible.
- **Pareto Chart:** The 80/20 rule is derived from this, separating the critical few from the trivial many (80% of your issues are usually caused by 20% of your problems).
- **Histogram:** Used to see frequency distribution of your data.
- **Scatter Diagrams:** Used to see a correlation between two variables.

- **Control Charts:** For visualizing and measuring process performance over time (run charts with limits).

I could go on and on about the importance of the quality of your products and services for much longer than this short overview, but that's too much to cover here, so let's leave it at this. At the very minimum, I can sum up what I would tell my younger self: *"Your focus on quality should be complete and methodical and will pay back mightily in your customer's loyalty and your bottom-line costs through the years."*

Some of the things I wish I would have known much earlier in my career that I know now, and I would like you to know are:

- Most **QA programs** are quality control programs in disguise without true quality plans and the quality engineering done on the processes to make it happen.
- **Quality control measures** need to be proactive and let you know quality issues are going to happen before they do or exactly when they do, so your reaction time is held to a minimum.
- **Quality of product** (QoP) and **quality of service** (QoS) are **equally important**, and both must be measured and proactively controlled at all times!
- The **hidden costs of quality failures** always, always, always cost more than the cost of failure prevention to begin with.
- **Your response to a quality failure is as important,** and sometimes more so than the quality issue itself.

The Importance of Customer Service

I know this sounds like something very simple, but I always find it fascinating how many organizations fail to realize this or keep this in front of them. As you can see from this graph here, your customer service or quality of service (QoS) is more important than ever.

The Many Needs of the Modern Consumer

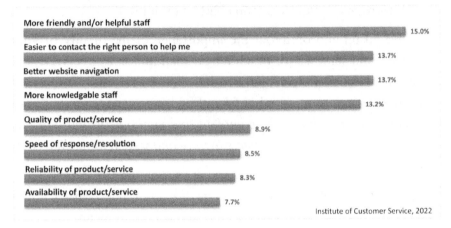

More friendly and/or helpful staff — 15.0%

Easier to contact the right person to help me — 13.7%

Better website navigation — 13.7%

More knowledgable staff — 13.2%

Quality of product/service — 8.9%

Speed of response/resolution — 8.5%

Reliability of product/service — 8.3%

Availability of product/service — 7.7%

Institute of Customer Service, 2022

In my career, I have seen and been part of companies that lose this focus in their day-to-day operations, slowly replacing their original focus on the paying customer with internal focuses on measures such as revenues, profits, inventories, etc., all things that, while important to running a business, are never as important as the actual products or services that touch the customer. How many times have you been in a local store where the owner or manager is focused on something other than their current customers in the store for whatever reason? How did that make you feel? How often have you had to wait unacceptable lengths of time on a chat or a phone call just to get a question answered by someone that you bought a product from? Not a good thing, right? You can feel that loss of customer focus, and I'll bet that eventually, it drives you not to purchase their product again if you have a choice.

Poor service to paying customers starts slowly from within for many companies, many times with simple missed internal commitments that then eventually snowball into missed customer commitments. How does this happen? Usually, it's because the people in an organization forget that the work they are doing should always be traceable to how it affects the customer. Product managers should be thinking about how much their customers love their products and how easy they are to use, not just how many products they have sold or what features they have. Sales managers should be aware of how high their customer satisfaction is and how that compares to their competitors, not just their sales revenues. Customer service managers should be measuring customer loyalty, customer friction, and customer turnover, not just how many calls they answer or the cost to service their customers. Constantly thinking like your customers and what they deem a successful outcome is the key to great customer satisfaction and is not that hard to do, as long as they remain your center of attention, always.

Here's a simple example of how a small measurement process breakdown in a company's shipping area can be an issue.

In today's business world, many companies measure their shipping performance daily (some weekly) but then report on that performance monthly (due to legacy processes and systems that reported it that way from years ago). That means an issue has a whole month to impact shipments before it is seen by the management team. Take into account the length of time it takes to find the cause of the issue and change the process or procedure to eliminate the issue, and you now have the potential of many months passing, with many shipments impacted, before the issue is resolved. It doesn't matter if we say we are working on it. What matters is that the issue has the potential to repeat itself every day if it is not solved.

To add some context to this, if you have a company that ships a thousand packages a month with a 98% on-time delivery rate, then that means twenty packages a month are delivered late. Now while that may not sound like a big deal and is the target for many manufacturing and shipping companies, it is to those twenty customers. Now, as your company grows and your shipments double, that's a very good thing, so your revenues have now gone up. The problem is that if all else stays the same, then your 98% on-time delivery now means forty customers a month are now experiencing late deliveries, and it goes on from there. The main issue here is that many operations and leaders in a company will be happy to report that their on-time delivery rate is 98% successful, but that means 2% of the time they were not, and depending on how big that number is, and how quickly the company is growing, that can become a big problem.

I have found over the years that the best approach to customer satisfaction is to treat every single service issue as a service failure and go after the cause of each with a mindset that even one failure is too many, just like pilots and surgeons approach their work. This mindset will eventually drive you towards zero defects, which is tough and, in many cases, impossible to achieve, but it is a good mindset to at least strive towards. A mindset that says errors are okay, up to a point, is one that will eventually snowball into larger issues developing and is one I do not recommend. History is littered with many companies that forget *it's always about the customer and the customer's experience* along the way.

- **Netflix** did not kill Blockbuster. Ridiculous late fees did.
- **Uber** did not kill the taxi business. Limited taxi access and fare control did.
- **Apple** did not kill the music industry. Being forced to buy full-length albums did.
- **Amazon** did not kill other retailers. Spotty customer service, lack of right product sizes and limited inventories did.
- **Airbnb** isn't killing the hotel industry. Limited availability and pricing options are.
- and finally… *Not being customer-centric is the biggest threat to any business.*

Customer service is the simple delivery of meeting your commitments, both product specifications, and service process. It is also meeting the customers' wants and needs, which are two different things. Customer needs are something they have to have because of their functionality. A customer *needs* a car with a trailer hitch because they *need* to pull a boat. Though any color of car with a hitch fits their need, a customer may *want* a specific color, say a white one (most popular car color), and they will make their buying decision based on both their need and their want. They will also *need* a specific delivery date, say in the spring, to pull a camper or boat to a vacation spot. So, to deliver on your service commitment, the car (need) and color (want), and date of delivery (need) are what you are committed to, and a miss in any of these three areas will be impactful and cause a customer service issue. Now, you can substitute a different color to meet the commitment, which will satisfy the needs, but in the end, if all three of the commitments are not met, then that is a quality-of-service failure and, thus, an unsatisfied customer.

So, to be great at customer service, what does it take? That's simple. Meet your commitments; don't commit if you can't meet them. Have what the customer wants to begin with. Here's a simple question to ask yourself every day:

"Do I have the right product or service at the right place, at the right time, and at the right price or value, having made the process of doing business with us as easy and enjoyable as possible in the eyes of the customer?"

If the answer is yes, then you are well on your way to customer success!

The Importance of the Sales Process

Thinking of starting a business or maybe working to improve the one you are already in? Then you need to think about the sales process. Nothing happens in the business world without a sale, which is why according to a recent study by Gartner, more than 40% of roles in the business world have some type of responsibility in the direct sales process. Think about it, if you go into a local store, everyone in that store is a "sales" person, whether they have that title or not. The store owner is part finance person, part manager, part service-person, and 100% salesperson (yeah, I know the math doesn't add up, but you get the point). Without a sale, nothing "happens" in a business; thus, it's the process of selling that gets it all started. From selling your idea to investors to get your "start-up" funding to "ringing up" or "booking" the sale in your system, it's the sales process that begins to make your cash flow!

As I mention in the "Importance of Customer Service" section, customers have both "needs" and "wants," and a perfect sales experience fulfills both. An example of this would be when a person walks into a local store to buy a jacket because the weather is getting colder. Any jacket will fulfill the customer's "need" by solving their cold problem but having that jacket in the color they like fulfills their "want" and has nothing to do with solving the issue of them being cold. If the store does not have the color they want, this is where a "great" salesperson comes in. It is now up to them to reason that customer through the thought process that it is more important they solve their problem of being cold, and although having their favorite color is nice, it is second to solving the problem, and thus any color will do that. In the end, if the customer decides to buy a jacket that solves their problem, one that may not be their favorite color, but the salesperson helped them understand that the color they purchased is still a nice one, then that was a successful sales process closure, and you can thank a great salesperson for that.

Another way to look at needs and wants is to think of them as "makes sense" and "feels good." Years ago, while I was attending a consultative sales training program, the instructor said something that stuck with me. He said, "People buy something for one of two reasons; either it makes sense, or it makes them feel good, and if you can make your product or service do both, you'll have a competitive advantage that you can leverage daily!"—and when you can't deliver this, then this cartoon is what you may end up with.

© 2012 Ted Goff

"Every step of the sales process went perfectly except the part where the customer buys our product."

This process happens millions of times daily in many different variations but think about it. The real value of the sales process and the salesperson is in helping solve a problem the customer has. If the purchase did indeed solve the customer's problem, then that is what we call a successful transaction.

So then, why is it that many of us get frustrated when dealing with "sales" people or the sales process in general? Mainly, it comes down to buying something we didn't need or that didn't solve our problem, which leads to frustration with both. Too often, we buy something online that we thought would solve our problem, but it was misrepresented, and then the return process is not easy (returns are part of the sales process, too, believe it or not). Or it does solve our problem, but the color wasn't exactly right. Because there is no salesperson there to help us understand that the want part of our purchase is less important than fulfilling the need part, we return it because it wasn't exactly what we were looking for. With the level of technology available in business today, it should be easy to give a customer both, especially online.

Anyway, the principles mentioned in these examples can be expanded out into many different types of companies, both large and small, online or brick and mortar; it doesn't matter. What matters is that the sales process gives the customer what they need to solve their problem and makes them feel good by taking care of that psychological want. Also, do keep in mind that the order process itself, whether it is standing in the checkout line or trying to enter your payment information online, is all part of the experience and plays into the customer satisfaction "want" of a faster and better experience every time.

One last thing I do want to leave you with here. It has been my experience that the best people in the sales process are the ones that are the best listeners and question-askers. They know how to ask questions to get to a customer's real needs and thus solve the real problem. They understand that when they are talking, they are only repeating what they already know and trying to sell someone something, but when they are listening and asking questions, they can and will learn something that can help them better understand and solve the problems of the customer they are listening to.

The Importance of Great Teammates and Friends

Jim Collins in *Good to Great* and Larry Bossidy in *Execution* mention the importance of having the right people on your team and having them in the right roles. I would like to reiterate that here and also add the importance of working with and associating yourself with great people in general, in both your personal and professional life.

When I think of this, words like trust, commitment, courage, knowledge, and others that we brought up in the 3Cs come to mind. But also words like listening skills, empathy, lightheartedness, and energetic, to name a few more. The most important thing you can do is constantly make sure you have the right people in the right roles, all working together for the same outcome. Regardless of who works for who or who reports to who, when you are part of a team, leader or not, you must have the commitment and courage to constantly work with everyone on the outcome and to coach, counsel, and call out people (respectively of course) when they need it.

Also, keep in mind that along your journey, you are going to work with people that are not part of your company, but they are still your teammates because everyone in your supply chain is part of the extended team that helps you be successful. So, how you treat and work with them will impact your ultimate end goal. Too many times, I have seen entrepreneurs, managers, and other individuals treat indirect contributors to their success differently than their direct employees. In the end, this type of behavior will eventually lead to failure. I have also seen great examples where people have treated everyone in their business process chain as if they were all on the same team all the time, and the results have been remarkable.

The one last point I want to make here is the importance of having great friends to your overall career, business, and personal success. As you travel along your journey, it is much more fun and enriching if you have people to travel with along the way or share your stories with. People who make you laugh, understand you as a person (think 3Cs here), accept you as you are, and always have your best interest in mind are the most valuable friends and helpers you can have. Nothing is more powerful than a friend that will tell you the truth when you need it, even if it's not what you want to hear. As well, the ability to discuss anything with your friends will help you through your rough times. I cannot stress the importance of having these few close friends or advisors with you along your journey to make the ride more enjoyable and less precarious. So do make sure you invite some of them along for the ride because when people say it is lonely at the top, I say it doesn't have to be that way; they have made that personal choice!

To achieve *Better Outcomes*:

- Do you have a quality assurance plan that includes QP, QE, and QC for all parts of your business?
- Do you update your quality plan frequently?
- Are you delivering the right product and service to the right place at the right time for the right price?
- Would your customers say you are easy to do business with?
- Do you know your customers' real needs versus their wants, and are you addressing those?

Quality and Service are remembered long after the price is forgotten... what do you want to be remembered for?

... think about it.

Part II

Better OUTCOMES!

... they're about Operational Excellence in all that you do!

Chapter 4

Effectiveness
... is always 1ˢᵗ!

"Excellence is never an accident. It is the result of high intention, intelligent direction, skillful execution, and the vision to see obstacles as opportunities."

–Anonymous

If you have been traveling along with me on this journey so far, that means you should have a good idea of where you currently are, an understanding of where you want to go, and why. You have also laid out a strategic plan to get you there. Congratulations on your progress. We are now heading into what is referred to as the "messy middle" of executing your plans, or the "real work," as I like to call it.

In this part of our journey, we will now talk about getting better outcomes through **operational excellence**. The concept of operational excellence has been around since the early seventies and has had many definitions over the years. The one I like the best is: operational excellence (OE) is a methodology and thought process of striving for efficacy (effectiveness of outcomes) throughout organizational processes, with the end goal of OE being to ensure customer expectations are met in an efficient and continuously improving manner. In simple terms, this translates into OE being the way to deliver outcomes to your customers in both an effective and efficient way, which leads us to this chapter.

Before we move forward, I want to bring up a phrase I briefly mentioned at the end of Chapter 2, "doing the right things" always. While this is very important, the expansion I mention is to add another "right," and thus, the phrase becomes "doing the right things right." This phrase, which I sometimes just abbreviate as RTR, is a quick way to check on yourself, and what you are doing, and stay true to your set course. Let me now expand on this some more by introducing two new words, ones that I am sure you've heard before, but maybe not quite with the importance I am going to put on them. Those are the words **effectiveness** and **efficiency**.

Effectiveness: Successful in producing a desired or intended result that comes about by *"doing the right things."* Having the right strategy and objectives coming from the customer or industry needs that you have proven with data are the right things to do. Are you targeted at the right service levels, reliability, quality, price, etc., to begin with?

Efficiency: Achieving maximum productivity with minimum wasted effort or expense, or what I like to say is *"doing the right things right."* Meaning you have applied the correct methodologies, processes, automation, technology, targets, etc., giving you the final product/service outcome that meets and exceeds the customers' expectations and your commitments to them, along with meeting your shareholder commitments.

Now that you understand these definitions, anyone can see why they might be important to your success in both your personal and professional worlds. I am going to ask you to park the term *efficiency* right now, so we can dive deeply into the importance of being effective first! Then, in the next chapter, I will dive deeply into what efficiency is and why you need them both (to avoid drift and other issues), and how to optimize them to be successful.

Being Effective: *By Doing the Right Things*

Doing the *right things* is not as hard as it sounds if you stay focused on your strategic direction. And your strategic direction process allows you to adjust for changing markets and customer conditions at the frequency necessary to serve them and stay competitive.

Think of it this way, you are starting to execute your well-designed and targeted strategic plans. This means you have decided what targets to focus on and are aiming for the bullseye. Everything is going along well. You're happy, motivated, and moving along in a "directionally correct" way. I say "directionally correct" because, as we know, unforeseen circumstances will arise along our journey, which can cause you to have to deviate or take "detours" from your plans. Which is why a good business leader is one that is always looking "around the corner," trying to anticipate what is coming so they can prepare for it before it arrives. Now another opportunity arises.

So, what do I do? Do I stay focused on my first opportunity (target)? Do I switch to the second target? Do I try to do them both? All valid questions that you need to address as quickly as possible, and that's where the challenges of decisions arise. But hold on, now more opportunities arise.

Suddenly, the challenges of having to make new or different decisions around one new opportunity get multiplied by the number of new opportunities available, and the decision choices get multiplied exponentially. Now the real work begins.

The real work I refer to is going back to your strategic direction and plans and seeing if the original assumptions are still valid, which may, and should, lead you back to your original SWOT. All that prior work should be revalidated to make sure it applies to your new set of opportunities. Resist the urge to chase after these opportunities (what we refer to as "shiny objects") until you validate them with real data as quickly as possible. Otherwise, you risk chasing things that defocus you from all your original good strategy work, and thus you deviate from your intended strategic direction.

Now, while chasing "shiny objects" is not a good thing, what also tends to happen is the opposite. Many companies stay too rooted in their original plans and thus miss opportunities they should have gone after. This happens because they take too narrow a focus on their market, their products, their services, their competition, etc., and arrive late to many opportunities. In the technology world, many companies missed the movement of services to the cloud because of this.

One last issue that does arise when it comes to new opportunities being available to you... completely missing them all together. If your external view is not well connected and you are not sensitive to market and customer changes, then it is easy to miss a shift to alternate products or services, like moving to the cloud. You run the potential of becoming obsolete before you even know it. Therefore, constantly looking outside yourself and your organization for information is important to long-term success.

The real key to staying relevant in a changing world is to remain flexible, be diligent about what is going on, and stay connected to the *voice of the customer*, or VOC, which should always be your first and best line of information.

The voice of the customer means nothing more than what it says, hearing, sensing, gathering, analyzing, and doing something with your customer's input or voice. It means staying connected to your customer in any way, shape, or form that allows you to feel what they feel about you, your products, and your services. It is always looking to see if you can prove to yourself that your products and services are faster-better-cheaper and delivering the right things to them. While this sounds simple, it is easy to forget, especially when you are focused on the day-to-day running of your business, and the next thing you know, your sales or customer satisfaction is dropping.

If you think about it, sales numbers and financial performance are lagging indicators of how well you are executing on your plans. If your plans are no longer valid because of a shift in the external business or customer environment, then that means you're original SWOT is no longer valid. Since you used a SWOT to build your strategic direction, plans, and established the targets that you are working towards every day, you can imagine what can happen.

Being Effective: *by being Faster-Better-Cheaper*

In my greater-than-thirty years in the business world, there are three things that consistently come up year after year in almost all customer-focused surveys. Customers request businesses to deliver their products or services faster, better, and cheaper.

- **Faster:** If you are already giving me what I want (the correct product or service), then please provide it with less wait time or with more immediacy. An example of this would be when FedEx introduced overnight delivery, which really disrupted the US mail system. Who would have thought people wanted to have deliveries overnight? Then a few years later, along comes Amazon and Amazon Prime, and they built a multi-billion $$$ business on getting people what they want even quicker, in two hours in some cases, another missed opportunity by others.

- **Better:** The need for more or better product features, higher quality products or services, fewer errors in the ordering and delivery process are all things that your customers look at when comparing your products/services to your competitors. Delivering "better" products or services (which includes your own internal service processes that touch customers) is something your customers have expected over the years and can be a real competitive advantage or disadvantage, depending on how you perform here.

- **Cheaper:** "I am paying a lot for this product or service, I wish it gave me more value," or "for that price, I expect this…" are just a few of the comments you hear customers make in this important area. Being "cheaper" is not so much about the price of your product or service; it's the perceived value your customer is deriving from your product or service for that price that is important. Think about Amazon Prime and how you get "free shipping," which is not free since you pay a yearly subscription for it, but it is cheaper the more you order, and it includes free streaming and added features, so they get some *better* too!

- **Customer Delight:** At the intersection of being F-B-C is the "sweet" spot, what I call the area of customer delight. It is the highlighted area in the middle of these circles where if you can execute strategies that deliver outcomes faster-better-cheaper than your competitors and your previous performance will make all customers delighted!

Delight Customers by Making and Keeping Commitments

One of the ways to ensure Customer Delight is by making service level agreements (SLAs) with your customers. SLAs are a powerful way to show how much you care about your customer commitment and give you and your teams something to focus on daily. A great example of an SLA commitment to the customer is L.L. Bean's unwritten guarantee that you can return your product to them for twenty-five years for repair or replacement, also Orvis's and Filson's lifetime product guarantee, or some newer restaurant guarantees that say, "we will make it right, or it's on us!" Powerful statements, indeed!

Now while SLAs are great to have, the only thing I want to caution you on here is that if you are going to make these commitments, then you had better keep them. Nothing is worse than a broken customer commitment or one that your people know you cannot keep (like zero defects in all that you do). It erodes trust in you and your company, and since bad news travels faster than good news in today's social media-driven consumer world, it can really impact your business. What I recommend when you want to make SLAs to your customers is that you work with your team to see which are the most valuable ones to your customers, which ones will differentiate you from your competitors, and which ones you can make and keep.

Being Effective: *by being Agile*

You can barely pick up a business report or business plan today without seeing the word *agile* somewhere in the first page or two. Whether it is someone saying their business is becoming more agile or saying they are being more agile in managing their employees, or that they are pursuing an agile development methodology, they are all trying to reference the same thing, which is that they are trying to move faster than they have before.

So, with agile being such a buzzword in today's world, what does it really mean? Well, here's the basic definition that I love to use, one that states it in its simplest form.

Agile... *the ability to move quickly and easily.*

Ok, so like some of the terms we have used before, why is it something so simple can cause such angst inside companies? Well, that has a lot to do with "walking the talk" around the word, let me explain.

Doing agile to something, in other words, trying to make something quicker, more flexible, and nimbler than before, is what most businesses and people focus on. Though often talked about in the efficiency part of an operations work, it is more important when applied in the effectiveness area since your customers and your people feel the agility change, especially when it gives them what they need or want faster and better than before.

Now, let's look at an example of how trying to be agile can quickly go off the rails in a business. Let's say some data analytics on your customer feedback survey points out that your company takes too long to implement requested improvement changes to your online ordering processes, especially for features that they would like to have right away. Maybe these features are costing you customers because you don't have them.

The analysis says it takes you over a month to make any changes, and that is too long from the customer's perspective, so it sounds like the company needs to become more *agile* here, right? To fix this, you gather the team together to analyze the issue and decide you need to change the process for implementing customer-requested changes. You determine that the actual work needed to make the necessary changes will take forty hours, so you get the team right on it.

As your team begins working to make the changes, you realize that a few team members have vacations planned, so they will be missing for a few days. Then you realize another team has to evaluate your work to make sure it is compliant with regulatory requirements. Then you realize that there are other departments that need to sign off on the work. In addition, you realize there are wait times in-between each phase because people have other things to do, so your forty hours of actual work have now expanded to three or four weeks due to scheduling issues. This reinforces the VOC, and since you let it continue this way, you now run the risk of your customers moving to a competitor who has figured out how to do this quicker or maybe had what they wanted already. So, what happened here? Why are some companies caught in this cycle where they start off with great intentions to be more *agile*, but in the end, fall short on that delivery, has to do with the misunderstanding that ***agile is not something you do, agile is something you live and become!***

What do I mean by that? Let's look at that last example for some guidance. First, one of the tenants of *agile* is to have teams that are self-supporting and sustaining, meaning the team has everyone on it at the right time and place to do all the work necessary, with all the decision power needed, to get the job done. So, the minute they must go "outside" the team to get permission to do something for their deliverable or outcome, it has already become non-*agile* since they may have to wait for someone's permission. Often, that someone must be brought up to speed or educated on what they are doing, so that will slow things down.

Secondly, to become *agile* means that teams are not single-threaded, so a missing team member will not delay the project (many delays are caused waiting for someone to come back from vacation, especially senior leaders). Real agile teams have people who can do more than one job and fill in for the roles that do the process step to their left or right (sometimes referred to as upstream or downstream) so that if someone is sick or has an emergency, the work does not stop.

Third, true *agile* teams understand that all planned or unplanned work stoppages (company meetings, unplanned senior leader requests for information or reports, teammates need to be on an *agile* improvement committee—my personal favorite) are all workflow inhibitors and thus anti-*agile*. So, true *agile* is about keeping work flowing and non-value-added activities at a minimum so that all time is spent on delivering value to the outcome; anything else in that process is just not *agile*.

Why do I spend time here explaining this? Because I can't tell you how many times I have seen managers talk about how well their *agile* programs are progressing. To prove it, the team will present progress, so they can show you how well the team, and they, are doing. I shake my head every time I hear this because this means that the team, or even just its leader, must take time away from their work to report on their work. I have personally been part of some of these review meetings and must say I should have been more vocal in stopping them, but many a time, I just let it pass by, going with the leadership flow or DNA, which was wrong of me.

A true *agile* leader, living agile in everything they do, understands that *agile* is about getting things done, and anything that interrupts that is wasting time!!! They minimize meetings and interruptions to the ones absolutely necessary to get the job done! They do not request anything from their teams while they are working that may break their focus or is not helping them deliver their outcome faster and better! Finally, they learn how the team manages their work and can look up the work status on the same systems the team uses without interrupting anyone's workflow for information. They understand that forty hours of work can be executed in a week with a focused team, or it can be done in one hour a week and take forty weeks with teams that are continuously multitasking and not being driven with the agile mindset of getting things done!

Being Effective: *with Digital First Thinking*

Being effective by focusing on your environment, staying in touch with your customers, and always looking to be faster-better-cheaper than ever before are all ways to keep you focused and on track with your strategy and plans. And now, I would like to add one last focus: are you thinking "digital first" in all that you do? Because that's one of the things that is coming around the corner.

New business models are emerging daily that are leveraging these new digital capabilities (think social media, mobile access, et cetera). Thus, you need to look at applying this new digital capability to *how* you do things, but more importantly, to *what* you are doing. The new business models represent ways to connect and work with your customers in ways not thought of before. Such ways can capture more satisfied customers, think of Amazon Prime again and how one-day and two-hour delivery changed the whole market or how you can order something online and pick it up at the store nearest you, sometimes that same day.

These business models did not exist before, and they exist now because someone came up with a more effective way to do these things (really, this is nothing more than delivering your product to customers, which companies like Sears and JC Penney could do years ago, just not as fast). When I think "digital" first, it is from the customer's perspective of F-B-C again and how I can apply this new "digital" capability to do it. Another way to think about it is what a "perfect" customer experience would look and feel like.

If you have your own brick-and-mortar business or even an online selling business, the main reason a customer comes to you is to buy something you sell. Now, how many times have you not had exactly what a customer wanted, and thus, you missed that sale? Think about how that affects your customer satisfaction and your bottom line. Now reimagine this in a digital world... what new capabilities or models could be applied to solve this problem in your business?

How can you use data to ensure you have the right products and services available to the right customers at the right time and place, which is the focus of company supply chains? How can you capture the customer experience and see which ones were satisfied with your two-week product delivery wait time and how many just went to a competitor to get the same product? There are so many questions that were not asked in the past because the data wasn't available; now, they can be asked. Yet many people and companies still don't ask these important questions because they are not used to doing it and thus don't realize that they can get these answers in today's digital age.

Being Effective: *with a "living" Demand Plan*

One of the biggest challenges of being effective is making sure you have a well-thought-out demand management plan. What I am talking about here is what volume of orders, sales, and work you believe you will get and how you will handle deviations from that plan. This is not a detailed plan on how you will efficiently deliver to the demand plan you have, but more what you will do if the planned demand does not materialize or if too much of it does. How will you pivot to different products or services to sell? Do you have alternate products or markets laid out? How will you handle a product recall or service issue? How will you meet your promise or commitment of on-time deliveries if you have too many orders and insufficient inventory? These are all part of your effectiveness. For your demand plan to be successful, you constantly have to think in a proactive, predictive, and forward-looking way because your competitors are!

Staying Effective: *with the Right Measures of Success*

When executing your plans and working to ensure you are focused and effective, it is important to have minimal control metrics, so you don't overburden your effectiveness but know where you are at all times. I recommend having both actual performance measures and predictive ones so that you know what your customers think of your current performance, and you can predict what they will think of you in the future if you execute correctly. You also need measures to tell you how your competitors and your industry are doing in comparison to your measures so that you keep that outside focus and don't turn your attention inward, which does happen. Notice I headed this paragraph with having the right measures of success, not the most, because having too many is as bad as having the wrong ones, so keep it to the important few where possible.

Okay, so we've laid out how important being effective is within a business context, but what about applying that to accelerating your career and your life in general. How important is it in that context? By now, you can see that most of the processes we have discussed here in this chapter can easily and readily be adapted to an internal focus, and the same level of importance applies to both. As mentioned before, if you focus on what you love to do and are good at it, then being effective will be that much easier since you will look forward to doing it more and more. The harder thing to do is stay focused on an outcome you do not fully love or believe in, and thus you become easily distracted.

Remember to keep in mind that *doing the right things right* starts with *doing the right things,* which is the key to your effectiveness. So, review your focus and direction frequently and stay connected to your customers; otherwise, you may find yourself efficiently cutting down the trees in the wrong forest, and what fun would that be if you cut down pine trees but were selling oak furniture?

To achieve *Better Outcomes:*

- **Effective...** are you *doing the right things*, cutting the trees down in the right forest?
- Is your focus on being *faster-better-cheaper* leading to delighted customers?

- Are you living an *agile* lifestyle or are you just talking about it?
- Do you think digital first in all that you do or same old way first?

If you always do what you've always done, you'll always get what you've always got.

... think about it.

Chapter 5

Efficiency
... doing the Right-Things-Right!

"America's business problem is that it's entering the twenty-first century with companies, systems, and leadership, designed during the nineteenth century."

–Hammer and Champy

So here we are, or should I say still are, in that "messy middle" of operations, getting ready to dive into the part where operational excellence experts spend most of their time, which is in the world of operational efficiency. Why do they spend most of their time here, and why is the area of operational efficiency so important to you? Because efficiency has to mainly deal with the process of delivering on what you have chosen to be effective in, and thus, effectiveness without efficiency is a recipe for long-term disaster. Or think of it this way, if you have all the ingredients for a great meal, but you put them together in the wrong order and then cook them at the wrong temperature, and then deliver the meal late, you know where that will lead, regardless of how great the final outcome is. Then, suppose you must purchase new ingredients and start over. In that case, you can see how that would not be a good thing either, so lots of bad things can happen with inefficient operations, along with ineffective ones, as described by the underlying processes of delivery and quality.

In Chapter 4 on effectiveness, I introduced the term *operational excellence*, and we discussed its importance. I then introduced you to two very important words, *effectiveness* and *efficiency*. At that point, I asked you to put aside the word efficiency and all that it stands for, so we could dive deeper into effectiveness first. Now it's time to pick back up where we left off with efficiency. Here's a quick refresh of its definition.

- **Efficiency**: Achieving maximum productivity with minimum wasted effort or expense, or what I like to say is "doing the right things right." That means that you have applied the correct methodologies, processes, automation, technology, targets, etc., giving you the final product/service outcome that meets and exceeds the customers' expectations and your commitments to them, along with meeting your shareholder commitments.

Like effectiveness, I like to think of efficiency in simple pictures, something like this.

Right thing done right.   Right thing done wrong.   Wrong thing done right; cutting down trees efficiently in the wrong forest.

Being effective is about choosing the right target to hit. Being efficient is hitting it consistently in the same spot with the least amount of shots and effort.

As you can see, there are multitudes of ways to accomplish what you are looking to do. The thing to always keep in mind, the thing you have to make sure you establish upfront, is that you are shooting your arrows at the right target to begin with because, as the old saying goes:

"There is nothing more wasteful and demotivating then making something efficient that has little value to the customer and shouldn't be done at all!"

So, are you still in the right forest?

One last thing I want to leave you with here in our introduction is the power of getting that outside perspective on your operations and their processes, just like making your ASA, gathering information through respected third parties and partners on your operations to get an **accurate operational assessment** (AOA) can quickly give you unbiased data and analytics on where you are doing well and where you have room for growth and improvement. I highly recommend getting an assessment like this if you haven't done one already; nothing like a fresh set of eyes on things to uncover hidden opportunities!

Being Efficient: *by doing the Right Things Right*

We have lots to cover in this chapter so let's get started because "doing the right things right" is where many businesses, and careers, are made or broken.

Jumping right into it, when it comes to efficiency, you should always think about achieving maximum output with minimum wasted effort and expense or input, which is a simple formula that looks like this:

Operational Efficiency = Output (Y) / Input (X)

Operational efficiency is an important performance indicator for any business; in many ways, the most important one right after making sure you are focused on the right things (remember, effective first) and are meeting customer commitments. It lets you know if you're engine room is functioning to your strategic plans and targets.

Companies, both large and small, tend to focus on improving operational efficiency regularly through means like process redesign, process standardization, and process automation (robotics and intelligent automation). Also, they have learned to keep in mind that it is not only about the financial performance of this equation but also having measures in place around it to tell them other things.

Things like process times, quality yields, etc., are all things that we will now discuss deeper as we look into something called systems thinking.

Systems Thinking

Systems thinking is thinking that looks at everything, especially business processes, in a connected, cause-and-effect way. The basic definition of systems thinking is a way of making sense of complexity by looking at the relationships of each piece or component of a process or *system* and how they interrelate with each other. It is represented in the simple formula of Y=fx's. In this formula, Y (the outcome) is a function or culmination of all the X's or inputs that connect to it. I will expand upon this more later in this chapter.

In the business or "operational" world, systems thinking is the ability to see and/or design the underlying capability needed to deliver the outcome. We use systems thinking in our everyday lives, yet we don't know it because we rarely think about the processes we execute daily to get things done. Think about something as simple as "building" your dinner for tonight. The first thing you must decide on is the "outcome" you are looking for. What type of meal? What time do you want it ready? How many people are you going to feed? What special dietary requirements do they have? This description makes up the Y. Then, to deliver this Y, you think about what "ingredients" you need to build it, how much they will cost, and when you need to procure them, so you have time to deliver the Y. These are your X's or input. Finally, you decide on what cooking "process" you will use to convert these ingredients into the final *outcome* (dinner). It is very important to spend time on the process design here because, as you know, you can cook ingredients in an oven, on top of the stove, in a microwave, in a pressure cooker, et cetera. So, there are many ways to convert your ingredients to the desired outcome, each with its own different process steps.

As you can see in this simple example, systems thinking can have a lot of complexity to it, but we never think about that because it is something that most of us do every day. Whether it is making a meal, getting our children ready for school, or even just exercising, there's always an outcome we are looking to deliver that needs process steps and inputs to get it done. The real power of systems thinking is in understanding that there are many X's that affect your outcome, and they can all contain variations in some shape or form. So how well you understand all your X's, plan for them, and control their variations defines how well your outcome will meet your or your customers' expectations. Now, let's look at a simple model I use that shows how systems thinking can be applied.

Being Efficient: *by doing things the Right Way*

The Input-Process-Outcome (IPO) model

As you strive for operational excellence by being operationally efficient, one of the first things you must do is develop the process steps (the X's) to deliver the outcome (Y) you are looking to achieve. Whether you are working on something complex, like building a house or a new product, or something simple, like pulling together your dinner menu, the beginning should always be the same. It starts with an understanding of what the **outcome** is you are looking to deliver (product, service, or dinner), figuring out what **inputs** are needed to deliver that outcome (order information, ingredients, et cetera), and then having a **conversion process** (called production, manufacturing, or cooking) to get it done, thus IPO! This is your complete "system," and a diagram of that would look something like this:

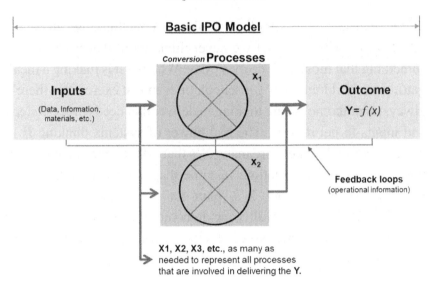

Each of these areas **(input-process-output)** has its unique challenges and opportunities. They also have commonalities, like the need for connected real-time data as much as possible and the need for feedback loops, as well as a focus on the output being faster-better-cheaper. You may have noticed that there are some X's and a Y located on the diagram, and these lend themselves to a simple equation that I briefly mentioned already, and you probably learned in algebra years ago and have forgotten; that being $Y = fx1 + x2 + x3 + xn$. This a very important piece of systems thinking because what it is saying is Y (the outcome) is a function (f) of all the X's that contribute to it; that's it. Simple equation indeed, but it's in the designing and/or discovery of the X's that contribute to the outcome, and knowing how they all integrate, where the challenges are. So now, let's take a deeper look at each area.

O is for OUTPUT or OUTCOME

So why start with the last letter, or *outcome*, rather than the *input*, which is where everyone likes to start? That's because all good system designs start with the end in mind since that is where your customer is and what your *outcome* needs to be designed for. This is called working from the "outside" in, and I cannot stress how important this is and how many times this gets forgotten by companies big and small. Very much like the previous example about building a meal, a well-defined outcome is the first step in building a successful process to deliver it.

Think about it. You've heard people say that to get better, you need to have well-defined goals, objectives, et cetera. Well, that's the same with any process. To make it the best it can be and design it correctly, you have to know what the outcome is you are building it for, and I am not just referring to some esoteric description like a dinner, or a car, or a house, but the detailed version that includes the type of dinner or car or house. In the example I used about cooking dinner, can you imagine if you didn't know what type of dinner (seafood, steak, vegetarian, etc.) you had to prepare? Your first issue would immediately be what type of ingredients to buy if you don't know the details of what type of meal you are building? And even if you know the type of meal, what if you don't know the time it has to be done by, or how many people will be at the meal… see how variation in the final deliverable can creep in there. Now, this is a simple example. Imagine what happens to your list of inputs (X's) when you add in the requirements from government regulatory agencies, state agencies, and even different country agencies; it can get quite complex indeed!

Examples of what I call product or service "*outcome* specifications" are the ones that the customer needs, the ones you deliver for them to be satisfied. These are usually the outcome specifications you and the customer agreed on beforehand. Now, the challenge begins because putting together processes and capabilities to build and deliver something you may have never done before is quite difficult, to say the least. Identifying the Y is not complicated, it's identifying and managing all the X's where things get difficult.

One quick note, if you notice, I use the word *output* or *outcome* interchangeably for this step in the model. Companies refer to goods as *output* and services as *outcome*. More product companies are also moving to this *outcome* nomenclature daily, so they can include the service component of their final deliverable and thus better represent their total customer experience.

P is for PROCESS

You know what product or service you need to deliver, you know when, where, and how much of it you need to deliver, and you have all the materials to build it and deliver to commitment, so now it's time to get it done. Simple, right? What could go wrong with that? Nothing, right? Ha, well, as anyone who has ever worked inside any process knows, plenty. Even in the simplest of processes like making a meal. Have you ever overcooked something, burnt the rolls, overcooked the lentils, or delivered an undercooked burger? Yep, I'm thinking you have all "been there, done that," so you know that even with the simplest of processes, guaranteeing and delivering a perfect product and experience is really hard to do. That's why quality control is so important in anything (output/outcome) that is going to be delivered to a paying customer. To explain this step even better, let's expand the model for this step.

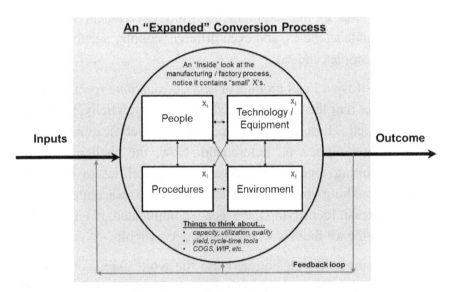

The conversion process (production, manufacturing, build process) is where the *inputs* come together, along with the well-defined *outcome* requirements (Y), and all of this is transformed into a "finished" good or service.

Terms like production plans, material plans, quality assurance, COGS (cost of goods sold), capacity, utilization, WIP (work in progress), etc., all come into play here. We could spend hours and chapters on each of these terms, but let's suffice it to say that they are all important, but we will not be covering them in this book. We will stay on the higher-level terms I have noted in the expanded diagram.

Looking at this expanded diagram above, you can see I have broken the requirements box into four distinct interdependent boxes (or small X's as I like to call them), those being:

- **People:** The labor and life blood of running the conversion processes and getting the outcome delivered. Make sure you have the right amount, the right type, and the right knowledge level at the right time and place. This also includes the right leadership that enables the people running the processes to be successful, not disables them.

- **Procedures:** Work instructions for each step in the conversion process. Usually includes work time and level of expertise to complete.

- **Technology and Equipment:** What the people use to get the job done. Old, outdated, or sub-par technology and equipment are some of the biggest productivity wasters there are, so be aware of your investments here.

- **Environment:** Work locations, facilities, and leadership are the key things to think about here, especially leadership!

Procedures for running the processes are, as I mention above, nothing more than work instructions, and they are extremely important. Think about it, at home, when we go to bake something, we will normally pull out a cookbook to read the directions to deliver the outcome we are looking for (ever baked a cake from memory, not that easy, is it?). In an IPO model, the *process* step requires some serious procedure design to make it all run smoothly. Steps that can help you deliver your outcome consistently every time to "delight" your customer. To make sure you are doing this consistently, the two questions you must continuously ask yourself are: "How well do I know what product or service I am delivering and how well do I know the process and procedures that deliver it?" "Do I truly understand what that process looks like, have visibility into how each step of that process is working on an ongoing basis, and understand the procedures necessary to get the work done, or do I rely on emails and institutional knowledge to tell me how things work?" The issue with any process, and its procedures, is that over time it will change, mainly due to the original designers and process operators moving on, and thus the new process operators, especially at the managerial level, start to change the original process for multitudes of reasons. Thus, the process integrity, and control of outcomes is lost. This is why having the procedures documented is so important.

I is for INPUTS

When I refer to *inputs* to an IPO model, I am referring to the information needed to deliver the final *outcome,* along with the labor, material, and other things needed that the *process* step will consume. From your original *outcome* design, you need to understand the details of the final product or service being delivered (Y) and the steps being built to deliver that (X's). From that, you derive the needed information to run the processes and the required materials and resources to get that done. The final step is to meet the end commitment to the customer. Where this gets tricky is in adjusting to changing product or service requirements, along with customer order changes themselves. When you have multiple products and services, along with multiple customers, keeping track of all the change requests from both of these areas is a daunting task, one that needs to be communicated and managed from the customer all the way back to your lowest tier supplier. This is where today's newly designed enterprise resource planning (ERP) systems are worth their weight in gold if implemented correctly. They allow you to connect the type of information you need to manage all of this complexity, starting from the *outcome* (customer) and threading all the way back to your suppliers.

As mentioned in the last chapter, I cannot overstress the importance of an active demand management process in your *input* step. Customer demand changes daily, and the best way to handle those changes is to know about them and in some cases, anticipate and predict them before they even happen (a great place for the use of artificial intelligence [AI] and predictive analytics). The faster accurate and complete order information is transferred to your *conversion process* team, the faster they can adjust their production schedule and thus keep inventories to plan. So, in summary for this area, here are the key pieces of operational information you need in this *input* step.

- **Customer Order Information**: Also referred to as demand information. What, where, when, how much, and any special requests, instructions, changes, or adjustments. This information will then drive the inputs needed for the procurement team.

- **Procurement Information:** This information comes from the order information and the production plan (usually derived from the mix of prior years' sales and recent forecasts). Buyers use this information to procure materials at the right time and place for the production team. In a high-functioning supply chain, the real-time flow of customer ordering information actively adjusts your materials ordering amounts, so there is no excess material sitting around that costs money. This is where connectivity of data is key, and by that, I don't mean spreadsheets that are shared weekly or monthly. I mean real-time sales and delivery data that let everyone know what has been sold, what has been ordered, how that compares to the production plan, and what immediate adjustments need to be made to ensure all is optimized and in sync. In today's business world, it is referred to as an IBP (integrated business plan), which is much easier said than done! You need to constantly know if you will have the right materials at the right place and time and not run out of them. Oh, and don't forget the right cost too.

- **Conversion Process Information:** Most of this is contained in the above, and it is the timing of the above information that is most important here. The delivery times of both the materials and the customer order must be synced to meet customer commitments.

The Feedback Loop or Loops

While not specifically called out in the acronym IPO, one of the most important pieces of the IPO model is the feedback loop. The FL, as I call it, is the path in which data or information (processed data) flows back to the previous step that delivered it. Why is this important? Becomes it allows each step in the process to see how their work was perceived by the next step in the process, all the way to the outcome, which would be the customer. Starting with the customer and working backward, you want to know the quality of product (QoP) information like whether it worked, met product specifications, was easy to use, et cetera. Then your quality of service (QoS) information, like whether it arrived on time, in the right quantity, and are you satisfied with everything? Each one of these data points can then feedback to the prior step to let them know how they met their customer commitment or didn't, which then starts the improvement cycle. In today's world, we are inundated with requests to rate the service we receive from our suppliers. Some would say too many requests, but they are all in the name of seeing how they did so they can do it better next time around, and it is all due to having and using well-designed feedback loops.

Now, let's look at our original IPO model with some of the operational information that we just covered added. This expanded IPO model should give you enough information to get started on one for your own business or business area, and then you can process map with much more depth from there.

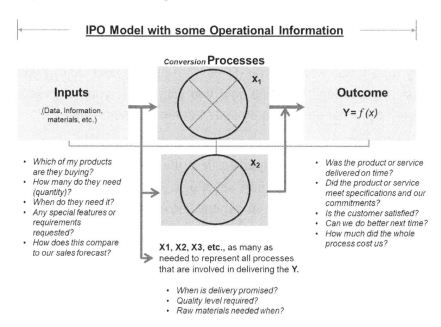

how how how how how
IPO Model with some Operational Information

Like I said, this is our original IPO model with some added information on what to think about and what questions to ask at each of the steps. Hopefully, you will find this useful in guiding your day-to-day thinking and developing your metrics to keep it all running smoothly.

Lastly, do keep in mind what I mentioned before, that it is the "outside-in" view of this process that is the most important to remember so you can stay externally focused on the customer. This is what many companies forget about and why you hear people say they have lost focus of their customers' needs. It always starts and ends with the customer, which means the flow starts outside, loops around, and then ends outside too. So, always start with the outcomes feedback data (since that is what the customer "feels") and work backwards from there. It is also important to remember that at the end of the day, positive Outcomes (Y's) are more important than Activities (X's) to customers, but this shows that if you focus on the X's you can usually guarantee the Y's outcome.

Being Efficient: *make your processes flow!*

Now that you have a good picture, or model, of your process from a very high level, what do you do next? Well, the next step in your "systems thinking" is to see how you can enable your process to "flow." So, what do I mean by that? Let me explain further.

Flow is defined as "the action of moving along in a steady, continuous stream." It is used to describe how rivers move, how work processes progress, how meetings go (yes, sometimes they actually do), and how life in general moves along. Flow is about ensuring that your process moves things along with the minimum number of interruptions possible and in the shortest time possible so that the outcome is delivered and your revenues and yourself grow. So how can you use this powerful word and put it to use in your professional life every day? Well, that's in looking at how you enable or disable flow in your IPO model.

Here's a list of some of the enablers and disablers to flow in a process, mainly identified in a work process way. This is by no means a complete list of them, just ones to get you thinking,

Flow Enablers:

- Clear understanding of what is valuable to the customer and prioritization of work by value.
- Work broken into smaller pieces and shorter timelines.
- Resources available right when they are needed.
- Focus on delivery of outcome, not distractions.

- Timely delivery learning reviews and adjustments.

Flow Disablers:

- Confusion on what needs to be delivered when.
- Not having work pieces arranged in proper sequence.
- Resources not available at the right time and place.
- Resources that do not have the proper training.
- Too many work interruptions (non-value-added meetings).

So, looking at these, where do you stack up? Are you enabling your processes and the people that run those processes to flow their work, or are you a disabler that causes decreased productivity along the flow? Something to think about.

I would be remiss if I didn't mention and give credit to Taiichi Ohno here, from whom many flow ideas originated. He is known as the "father" of the Toyota Production System (TPS), which was the precursor to the Toyota Way and the fourteen principles they developed at Toyota back in the early seventies. Toyota used these principles to become one of the best auto manufacturing companies in the world, with the highest rated quality, by putting continuous flow principles to work there. I do recommend you research these amazingly ahead-of-their-time principles further when you get a chance; it will be well worth the investment of your time.

Now that you know what flow is and how to enable and disable it, the next step is to think about if flow happens continuously.

Overall, the purpose of having a great IPO model is to allow you to create a continuous "flow" capability that delivers value to your customers, where everything moves smoothly from one stage to the next. This means moving from the sales process through the order process to the order fulfillment process (which would include the conversion process) and finally to the delivery process (part of the output process step). When all this is running smoothly, or "frictionless," your customers will be getting what they wanted when they wanted it and how they wanted it, and you will have achieved operational excellence!

Being Efficient: *by continually improving performance*

Doing a quick look at our journey so far, we surmise that we know where we were, know where we are going, have set our goals and objectives to get there, and have designed our simple IPO model to follow to move us along and keep us focused. So, our next step is to figure out a way to learn from and improve upon our processes.

The Japanese have a term for this called "kaizen," defined as "continuous improvement," always looking for a way to do things better. As I mentioned before, as we move along our journey, we will run into unanticipated events that will cause us to have to adjust or deviate from our plans... and maybe some of our end goals. But what if everything is working correctly and running smoothly? Does that mean we got everything right the first time, and there is no room for improvement? I say absolutely not. And why is that? It's because the knowledge that was available to you when you designed the IPO has changed. The next day there is new knowledge available in the world about the running of your system, which now makes your knowledge a day old and maybe even dated. I know this sounds harsh, but it's not the day-later timing that is the issue—it is the year(s)-old knowledge that was used and hasn't been updated since. That is the issue.

When Hammer and Champy made the statement I led this chapter with, *"America's business problem is that it's entering the twenty-first century with companies, systems, and leadership, designed during the nineteenth century,"* they were just pointing out that so many of today's processes and systems were designed decades ago, yet they are still being used today. Does that make sense with the knowledge and new capabilities that have been introduced since then? Think of how much power we have in our mobile devices today and how many companies are still not taking advantage of those capabilities on an ongoing basis.

The real problem or opportunity here is that many companies are **currently successful with these older or aged systems, sometimes referred to as legacy debt, and** have a false sense of security built around that. They have convinced themselves that the newer technology is not for them, or they wait to see how others use it before they decide what to do. Thus, many of them eventually end up left in the scrap heap of failed corporations because they didn't have discipline in their operational processes to prevent them from becoming inconsequential to current or future customers.

Remember, whether that discipline was in staying connected to their customers and designing their products and services with the right value, to begin with, or using that information to improve the processes that deliver their current products or services to the customer faster-better-cheaper than before, it doesn't matter. What matters is that they missed the opportunity because they weren't continuously looking to improve themselves each day. What really matters is that their thinking does nothing more than reinforce a famous quote attributed to Albert Einstein *"The definition of insanity is doing the same thing over and over again and expecting different results."* I ask you, how often are we doing that same thing?

Continuous Improvement Methodologies and Tools

So, how do we prevent that from happening? Something I learned as a new engineer at Hewlett-Packard was to have a continuous improvement mindset, one rooted in improving things by using a simple cycle of defining, measuring, analyzing, improving, and controlling (DMAIC). It is a data-driven improvement cycle used for optimizing and stabilizing business processes and designs.

DMAIC at a glance

DEFINE	MEASURE & MAP	ANALYZE	IMPROVE	CONTROL & CLOSE-OUT
Understand the issue and set the context	Baseline current process performance	Understand the causes & effects	Develop options, make choices, then implement	Plans to sustain Improvements

DMAIC is a core tool used in an improvement methodology called Six Sigma. However, it is not exclusive to that methodology, and I have found it useful as a framework for all forms of continuous improvement initiatives. I define it as a data-driven strategy for improving processes. Let me briefly expand on each piece of the cycle.

- **Define** is the first step; it's where you clearly state the business problem and issue. Stating the issue, not a symptom, is the challenge here. Seek to clarify facts, set objectives, and add the VOC (voice of the customer) here. This definition can also be used to add something new, not just fix a problem.

- **Measure and Map:** This is the data collection step. Here is where you collect current performance data and artifacts around the current business processes and its current performance. Make sure you identify all the processes (X's) contributing to the Y here and have all available process maps. If the maps are not available, then they will need to be created and usually take the longest time. If there are maps available, they need to be validated for currency.

- **Analyze:** The purpose of this data-driven step is to identify, validate, and select the root cause to fix. Use of a fishbone diagram is very helpful here. Causality is looked for here, as well as correlation; high-quality and relevant data is key.

- **Improve:** Identify, test, and implement a solution to the problem or issue. Can be a partial or complete fix. Experimentation and hypothesis testing are key here. True improvement comes from looking for opportunities to…

- o *Simplify*... eliminate, consolidate, and streamline
- o *Standardize*... where variability doesn't create value
- o *Automate*... where possible, especially repetitive steps and multiple handoffs. And remember, just because something can be automated doesn't mean it should be, some things are done better manually.

- **Control:** After the solution is implemented and proven to work, control metrics are engaged to ensure the sustainability of the fix or "make it stick," as we say, and give immediate visibility if it doesn't.

- **Close-Out Review:** Where we talk about lessons learned in delivering this initiative and then get ready for the next opportunity.

As you can see from the layout of the steps above, over the years I have tweaked them and added a few things, like adding another M (map) and another C (close-out), so I really think of this as DM^2AIC^2 just to try to make it as complete and useful as possible.

Also, as I briefly mentioned here, the DMAIC cycle is very close to the **seven-step scientific method** many of us learned in school. If you think about those steps (observe the issue, state the issue, perform research, develop hypothesis, test hypothesis, collect and analyze data, draw conclusions), you can see how closely they resemble DMAIC and understand this thought process has been around a very long time. It is simple and key to solving problems and taking advantage of opportunities without overcomplicating things. It also helps you to focus on "fixing the problem," and not "fixing the blame," which happens many times as many of you probably have already seen.

What is Six Sigma?

As I briefly mentioned in this past section, DMAIC is often referred to as part of the Six Sigma methodology, which is really nothing more than a collection of techniques and tools for process improvement, especially centered around improving accuracy. It was introduced by engineers at Motorola Corp. back in the late eighties. Six Sigma originates from the statistical modeling of processes and refers to the yield of defect-free products or services. Six Sigma means less than 3.4 defects per million of products produced, which is a performance of 99.999% perfection to a million, sometimes referred to as Five Nines.

What is Lean?

Lean and lean thinking was born out of the Toyota production system (TPS) that I mentioned earlier. It is a transformational framework that aims to provide a new way of thinking about how to organize activities in an optimum way so that you eliminate any "waste" or non-value-added activity in the steps of the process. It uses the concepts of customer value, the streams that deliver that value, flow, pull, and perfection as its main tenants to increase speed in a process. The basic thought behind lean thinking is that if you train every person to identify wasted time and effort in their own job and how to improve processes by eliminating this waste, the resulting culture will deliver more value to the customer quicker and at less expense, thus developing the team's competence and ability to work better together.

What is Lean Six Sigma?

As you can see, lean and Six Sigma are two powerful methods that can help anyone become better in the continuous improvement of their processes. However, the real power of these two methods is displayed when you combine them to solve problems since they are very complementary in their approaches. We call this integrated methodology Lean Six Sigma, abbreviated as L6S.

	Lean	Six Sigma
Goal	Improves process speed by removing inefficiencies through the process, end-to-end.	Reduces variation and improves quality at each step in the process.
Focus	*Identifies non-value-added process steps and other wastes that cause delays.*	*Uses DMAIC with quality tools to eliminate variation.*
Method	*Flow improvement through value stream mapping, waste reduction, and kaizen events*	*VOC, deep data, statistical variation identification, and elimination.*
Result of L6S	Lean speed + Six Sigma accuracy delivers higher quality at a lower cost with increased customer satisfaction, think F-B-C!	

As you can see from these descriptions, both these methods focus on eliminating variations in outcomes and quality and improving customer satisfaction by increasing speed and reducing waste, so I thought we would take a moment and discuss what waste is a little deeper...

Waste

Waste, by definition, is "to use or expend carelessly, extravagantly, or to no purpose," which is pretty easy to understand. In lean thinking, "waste" is commonly defined as any action that does not add value to the customer or, in other words, something the customer would not pay for. It is usually defined as "wasted" or unnecessary steps in a process that do not benefit the customer. There are seven well-defined "wastes" in lean Six Sigma, and they are...

- **Inventory:** Excess materials or labor, people or inventory waiting to be used to make your product or service.

- **Motion:** Too many steps or too much paperwork, poorly designed work steps or area.
- **Overproduction:** Producing excess of your product or service that does not sell when completed.
- **Overprocessing:** Adding more features than the customer wanted or needed, think non-value-added features.
- **Defects/rework:** Anything that has to go backwards in the flow of your IPO process, whether to fix (quality issue) or adjust (feature issue).
- **Transportation:** Moving things from one place to another, not having the right inventory in the right place (warehouse or store) when needed.
- **Waiting:** This is the main productivity killer, and the reason most processes are less than 10% efficient, meaning 90% of the time they are waiting for something (approval, materials, changes, labor, et cetera).

...and I like to add an eighth one, **Underutilized Human Resources**. Not using your team to its full capacity and real capability or using the wrong level of expertise in a work process will harm efficiency.

So, as you can see, when you start to look for opportunities to improve your processes, there are many "wastes" to keep in mind and look for. The challenge is finding your biggest wastes and dealing with them in a prioritized order of their impact to your operations and outcomes. Most of the time, you will have many of these wastes in your systems, not just one or two. I also recommend, like always, that you work from the outside back into your processes, starting with my defects on deliverables, mainly because a failed product or service is what customers feel most. After starting there, I immediately go after my wait time because this is such a killer of productivity, can sometimes actually be the cause of defects, and can improve both morale and costs in an instant on improvement. So, since wait time is such a big opportunity, let's talk more about it or what I call the "disease of waiting."

The "disease" of waiting

I like to refer to wait time as the "silent" productivity killer. It creeps into a well-defined original process over time and slowly erodes speed in all aspects of a company. From slow product or service delivery to slow decision-making, to slow customer responses, to slow employee hiring and onboarding, wait time can undermine your entire process. It is something that large companies convince themselves they just must live with over the years, and small ones use this thinking for a competitive advantage. How many times have you heard small companies being called nimble or agile? Speed is what they are referring to. Here are just **a few symptoms** of the "disease of waiting" in a company...

- Decisions take too long.
- Windows of opportunities are missed.
- Deliveries and outcomes are put on hold when a team member can't make a meeting or is out (sick, vacation), so customer commitments are missed.
- New hires are lost to competitors that made their offer faster.
- Meetings that end with another meeting as the outcome rather than a decision or where the presentation wording is more important than the content.

Recently, Google's CEO, Sundar Pichai, implemented a new internal company strategy based on three questions that he hopes will bolster productivity among his employees. The three questions were: *What would help you work with greater clarity and efficiency to serve our customers? Where should we remove speed bumps to get better results faster? How do we eliminate waste and stay entrepreneurial and focused as we grow?* As you can see, all topics we discussed in this chapter, but more importantly, two of these are directly related to moving faster or eliminating wait time, so you can see how important this topic is to some of the largest companies in the world.

What causes much of the wait time outlined above? Well, the "root causes" are varied and many. It can be that the company has been or is operating in a regulatory environment, which means that they may have to wait for government approval on things (airline and pharmaceutical industry) which takes time. Or it may be that the DNA of the company has always been like that, never putting a premium on moving fast in their business vertical until recently (because the speed of business has picked up for everyone in the last five years). Regardless of each company's individual reasons for allowing wait time, here are just a few root causes of today's wait times that are common across most companies...

- Lack of well-defined or well-understood customer requirements or outcomes.
- Poor understanding of upstream and downstream needs of each other and the operational processes/procedures.
- Too much specialization of work, not enough generalization (where teammates can alter roles and help each other out).
- Lack of resources (labor, material, time, or data) needed to get the job done!
- Risk-averse culture, leadership, or industry.
- Lack of focus on customer value.
- Lack of TRUST!!!

There are many, many more causes of wait time, but the one I want to expand on here some more is the one that can have the most impact on helping you deliver your product or service faster and better than before, the one that can improve your bottom line starting tomorrow is TRUST.

Trust is the one action that you can start tomorrow and grow as you go. Trusting your team, the people that you have hired to do what you hired them to do, and then asking them what they need from you to get their job done, is what I am talking about. Steve Jobs had a great saying when he was at Apple that went something like this, *"It doesn't make sense to hire smart people and then tell them what to do. We hire smart people so they can tell us what to do."* I have always loved this saying because it immediately smells of trust, trust in the people you've hired, trust in the process that hired them, and trust in yourself to allow them to do their job! Something to think about and keep in mind when you are trying to cure the "disease of waiting."

So, what can you do about the "disease of waiting?" Here are just a few ideas you should think about, most of them implementable right now, if needed!

- Start with increasing trust in your team or teammates tomorrow. Enable them to do their jobs, don't disable them.
- Insist on process simplicity, standardization, and automation in all that you do when it makes sense.
- Have meetings to solve problems, not to pass information or update people, there are better ways to do that without meetings.
- Give the team the resources they need to get the job done. And, if you can't give them all the resources they may need, then at least explain that to them and then work with them to figure out how to still get the job done.
- Train more, communicate more, and hold accountable more!

One last thing I want to mention that can help any company reduce waste and speed things up is don't reinvent the wheel each time you do something. Instead, leverage what has already been done. The lack of "reuse" or "leveraging" prior work is an area so many companies can improve upon. Companies, especially large and/or global ones, have already solved many of their problems, but they just don't know it because of a lack of knowledge sharing and learning. Thus, they solve it again and again, spending time and money wastefully each time. The simple process of leveraging and learning from past work by capturing it and filing it correctly, especially easy in today's data-driven world, would immediately reduce wasted time and speed up higher-quality results.

So that it doesn't seem that there are no companies leveraging their prior work, I'd like to call out and recognize one that does it exceptionally well, and that is the business consulting industry. Consulting companies have great databases that file the history of their client work and solutions globally, and thus, they can increase their level of success by looking at how someone else in their company has already solved a problem for another client around the world and then solve the next problem better. All businesses should think of using a knowledge depository just like this, not just consulting companies.

In ending this section on continuous process improvement tools and methodologies, I would be remiss if I didn't mention that there are many other methodologies you can apply to be successful at this. Some of the other methods, tools, and capabilities available that you've probably heard of are ones like kanban, kaizen, agile, waterfall, SAFe, and project management, to name a few. These methodologies are valuable to use at one time or another, depending on the scope and classification of your issue or opportunity. What I will say is this: be careful not to fall into the trap of trying to use the most recent tool you have read about or that some partner has told you about. Being good at process improvement is as much about knowing what methods, tools, and capabilities to use when as it is about identifying the right problem to solve. Getting either one of those wrong will lead you to failure in the end.

Operational excellence through excellent process execution

Getting back to our original storyline on how to become the best version of ourselves and our business, our process has gone something like this. We started by developing our SWOT to identify opportunities and what we wanted to focus on. We did a GAP analysis. From that, we developed our strategic plan and then our business plans, along with some of the other pieces to that plan. We then talked about making sure we chose implementation items for the strategies that were focused on delivering products and services to our customers faster-better-cheaper (FBC) than ever before. Then we focused our operational plans on being effective and efficient, using our people, processes, and technology (PPT) to get it done. And then, we discussed process improvement and the opportunities to use lean Six Sigma and other tools and methodologies to reduce wait times and other wastes that keep you and your teams from performing at your optimum level.

So, we started off this chapter by saying that effectiveness and efficiency were about doing the right things right, and now I'd like to finish it off with some thoughts around that...

Doing the right things right (RTR) will deliver operational excellence through superior process execution and outcome excellence, allowing you to deliver the right products or services to the right customer at the right time and place at the right price.

So, if you have the knowledge and discipline to choose the right things to do (effective) and then work to deliver them with well-designed processes and procedures run by well-trained and competent people enabled with the latest technology and great leadership (efficiency), then you have the recipe for success, period, so let's go get it done!

To achieve *Better Outcomes*:

- Are you doing the **Right Things Right,** and can you prove it?
- Do you fully understand your **IPO model** and are using the feedback information to solve bottlenecks and create flow?
- Are you doing the right things better today than yesterday, with an eye towards lean and eliminating the eight wastes in everything that you do?
- Are you applying continuous improvement methodologies like **DMAIC** to improve your processes?
- Do you know the difference between lean and Six Sigma and when to use each of them for maximum effectiveness.
- Do you have the **disease of waiting** or have you cured that once and for all?

There is nothing quite so useless as doing with great efficiency something that should not be done at all.

... think about it.

Chapter 6

Metrics, Targets, and Controls
... *Doing the Right Things Right and Proving It!*

"You can't manage what you don't measure."

and

"If you can't measure it, you can't improve it."

–Many People

In business today, we often find that we are very data-rich but extremely information poor. Thus, not allowing us to make sound business decisions as quickly as possible. Why is that, you ask? Well, the reasons can be varied. Still, mainly it's because we haven't really taken the time to figure out exactly what information we need to run our processes and what metrics, targets, and controls (MTC) will give us that information. So, what we do is measure or look at whatever we have on hand or can get right away and try to just use that information.

Sure, we have high-level outcome metrics like total revenues or sales per month, costs to produce them, expenses to sell them, etc., but do we really have all the details on the data underneath that level? Or an understanding of where it came from in our business processes so that when it is not moving in the right direction, we can understand that and adjust it before it impacts our customers? Do we know if the data we get for our presentations has been altered, changed, or processed along the way? Do we know how the targets we are trying to hit were developed or set? Do we know the actual time and date the data was taken or extracted from whatever the source system was? These are just some of the questions around data that need to be answered to make sure what you are looking at is high-quality, timely, and in the end, accurate and actionable. Without asking these questions upfront, it is easy to jump to the wrong conclusion, take or be led down the wrong path, and end up somewhere you don't want to be, all because the data pointed you in the wrong direction. So, to keep me on the right path, I always simplify the process of MTC into these three questions: "Am I measuring the right things? Am I measuring them the right way? And can I prove it?"

Bill Hewlett used to say, *"What gets measured gets done,"* and to this day, it is a statement that has lived the test of time. The only issue with this statement is that it leaves out one very important piece: if you measure the wrong things or have low-quality data, to begin with, then the measures will never give you what you really need to run yourself or your business. So, now let's dive deeper into what I mean by measuring the right things and then being able to prove it!

Metrics: *Can you prove you are doing the right things right?*

Measuring the right things

Makes sense so far, right? Who would want to measure the wrong things in any endeavor? Well, you would be surprised how often that happens. Just like starting with the outcome, or again, what is important to your customer, the best way to make sure you are measuring the right things is just to make sure they are impactful to your customers to start with. Measurements like customer satisfaction, on-time and complete deliveries, product stockouts (how many times have you wanted to buy a product in a store only to find out they didn't have your size or color?), and product returns all give you customer-impacting information that allows you to look at your processes and see where they need to be improved. We call these and others like these actionable measurements since the information gleaned from these measurements allows further analysis to be used to change something in your process, meaning you can take an impactful action on your outcome.

This is also a good area to think about your strategy overall: will the measures I am putting in place let me know if I am succeeding in my goals? Will they let me know if I am closing the GAP to where I am trying to get to? Again, these are some of the high-level metrics. The ones that are harder to come by but give you that actionable information I was talking about. The measures around faster-better-cheaper.

So, are you measuring these things? Are you executing your initiatives correctly? Do you have the data to prove that, or is it just opinion? What about your people-process-technology measures? Do you know how well your team is doing, not just in their process work, but as individuals? You undoubtedly know how your processes are working by now, but do you know which one of your people or teams is doing the great things? How about technology implementations? Do you know what people think of the new technology? These are all things you should think about. When you have as many answers as possible and know what you want to measure and why, I recommend you classify your metrics into three areas: reactive, proactive, and predictive. This will help you see if your metrics are actionable and how to use them to keep you on track and ahead in the game.

- **Reactive metrics:** Metrics that tell you what already happened, like a monthly sales performance or quality report. Needed, but it's like driving your car by watching your rearview mirror. It can be dangerous since what you are seeing has already passed.

- **Proactive metrics:** Metrics that give you information that you know in your industry is a good predictor of something that is going to happen next. Customer satisfaction measures are a good one here; if that is heading down, it is usually a predictor that your sales will soon follow.

- **Predictive metrics:** Similar to proactive metrics, but usually with added information derived from predictive equations (correlation and causality come into play here) that can be used to help you be better prepared for the future. Machine learning (ML) and artificial intelligence (AI) are being heavily applied here in today's world.

Why is it so important to make sure you are measuring the right thing, and interpreting those measures the right way? Here's a great example of why.

During World War II, fighter pilots would come back from battle with bullet holes all over their planes. In analysis of the patterns of these holes, the Allies initially thought the best course of action was to strengthen the areas on the planes that had the most holes or damage to them to increase combat survivability.

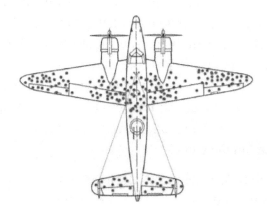

A mathematician, Abraham Wald, pointed out that perhaps the reason certain areas of the planes weren't covered in bullet holes was that the planes that were shot in certain critical areas did not return. This insight led to armor being reinforced on the parts of returning planes where there were no bullet holes, and this wisdom led to an increase in the number of planes returning from missions and in the ultimate saving of crew members' lives. It also led directly to aircraft design changes in the future.

What this shows is that the reason we are missing certain data may be more meaningful than the missing data itself. Measuring the right things, looking at them in the right way, and sometimes even listening and looking for what is not there are all important to your outcomes.

Measuring the right things right

Since you now know the importance of measuring the right things, how do you do it? Referring to the last example, just start with that outcome and customer (the pilot) and work back in (saving their lives). Think about the IPO model again and start with your output step. The diagram below shows the model again, along with some standard control metrics.

IPO Model with some Standard Control Metrics

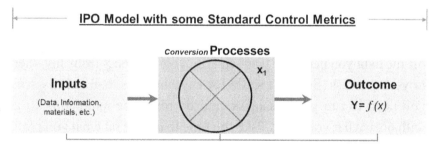

Order–Demand Plan and Performance questions to answer, so you need to collect this data	Build and Deliver Plan and Performance	Delivery and other Customer Impacting Performance Metrics
• Which of my products are they buying? How much of it?	• Demand Actual to Forecast	• Did we deliver on time?
• Are there special features they are asking for that we don't have?	• Labor allocation (capacity & utilization)	• Did product or service meet specifications and/or our SLA's?
• When do they need it compared to when do we offer it?	• Cost of Goods Sold (COGS)	• Did the product or service meet other commitments we may have made?
• Sales price compared to actual price (see discounts)	• Purchasing Management (cost of materials, vendor delivery time, quality)	• Is the customer satisfied?
• How does this compare to our forecast for sales?	• Inventory Management (how much do we have, where is it, actual cost to plan purchase cost)	• Can we prove the end-to-end quality of our delivery processes (cycle-times, rework, service failures, etc.)?
	• Quality of workmanship (rework and scrap, production yields).	• Can we do better next time?
		• How much did the whole process cost us?

When thinking about what touches your customer, think about what touches your finances, and think about what information you need to run each step. Do you have this information? What data is needed in each step to give you this information? Then think about where that data is and how you are going to get to it (what we call data access). Think more about the actual information you need BEFORE you try to figure out what data will give you that information. Often, the information you need is a complex equation that will require multiple different pieces of data to give you the information, especially in today's complex world, which is why there is such a dire need for more data engineers, data analysts, and data scientists.

A key thought to keep in mind here is the importance of taking the data from the right step or data point in your process. In the past, that was a problem, especially in manual or mechanical systems, since getting data while the system was running was difficult and possibly dangerous. But, with the advent of the internet of things (IoT) and other digital enablers, it has become much easier to pick off the data you need and want and run your business from anywhere in your process. So don't settle for anything less than exactly what you need to run your business, and do resist the temptation to go with only what you have. Take the time to decide on what you really need and don't need—you will be glad you did!

Targets: *Setting your Performance Goals*

You are ready to measure the right things and to measure them the right way, so now it's time to move on to setting the targets for those metrics so that you can measure your performance to them.

The first thing to understand about setting targets is that you need to know where you are today so that you can measure your direction and deviation from that point. Setting a growth target for sales or operational performance means you are baselined to some starting point, so make sure you have full faith in that starting point and that you know that it is accurate.

The next thing to understand about setting targets for your goals is that you need to take your time and do it correctly. Otherwise, you run the risk of going in the wrong direction right from the start. In setting up targets for your goals, a much-used industry acronym I have found very useful over the years is **SMART**, which describes the characteristics each goal target should have and stands for:

- Specific: Make your goals easy to understand, and as unambiguous as possible.
- Measurable: Describe the evidence that will prove you are making progress.
- Achievable: Your goal is reasonably accomplishable within a certain timeframe.
- Relevant: Your goal will align with your strategic plans and values.
- Time-Bound: A realistic yet ambitious end date.

I always find this a quick way to test the target numbers I want to strive for. So, if you have never used **SMART** before, you might want to give it a try. It's a quick litmus test that helps you set up your targeted goals correctly and helps keep you there.

Lastly, always remember that people will rally around tough to reach goals and their targets with the right leadership and incentives. So, take as much time as needed so that your people understand how your targets connect to your goals, why those goals are important, and what's in it for them if they reach those goals. This last part is something called WIIFM, which stands for "What's in it for me," and is important to remember as you explain your **SMART** goals to your team and others.

Controls: *How to keep your outcomes on track*

There are many ways to measure and control your outcomes, but the one I will refer to here I have used repeatedly in my career. It is called the balanced scorecard. I found this "layout" extremely easy to understand and use, and it's been my savior many times over the years. The balanced scorecard (BSC) is a management system developed by Robert Kaplan and David Norton in the early nineties. It is a system aimed at translating an organization's strategic goals into a set of performance objectives that can be measured, monitored, controlled, and changed, if necessary, to ensure that an organization's strategic objectives are met. The **BSC groups measurements into four main aspects of a business:** learning and growth, business processes, customers, and finance, which in turn helps businesses organize their measurements in a structured and connected strategic way. These groupings help you focus on the key areas that are important to any business, making it easier to measure and lead them. Here is an example of a generic business scorecard strategy layout, starting with getting your strategies in the right area. Then, the next diagram is the measurements and control sheet that would be the second part of the processes for active management of your targeted deliverables.

Keep in mind this is just one example of how to do this—there are many more available. Also, when putting together your program, make sure you design it for you and your business needs, not someone else's.

Balanced Scorecard

Financial	Maximize business value creation and revenues	Manage unit costs of operations by activities	Maximize business profit returns

Customer	**Effective** ◀▶		**Efficient**	
	High customer satisfaction	High quality services	Industry competitive cost structure	Faster, Better, and Cheaper than before

Business Processes

Operational Excellence

Faster, Better, and Cheaper than before and can prove it!	Online support times and quality	Lean Six Sigma initiative results
Reduction in process steps and complexity	Actively managed QoS and QoP	Improved process productivity	Use of emerging technology

Learning & Growth	Attract and retain talented staff	Foster career development	Promote a culture of customer service	Sustain skills in key technologies

Balanced Scorecard Control Template

	Strategic Goals	Initiatives	Measure	Targets	Results
Financial	1. Maximize business value creation and revenues 2. Maximize business Profits 3. Manage unit costs of operations by activities	1.1 Initiatives that support what you are going to do to deliver goal #1 and then #2, #3, etc. (may have multiple Initiatives for each goal so better to use 1 page for each goal area)	1.1.1 What are you going to measure when that shows this initiative is on track?	1.1.1 What targets are you going to achieve by when, how does it compare to where you currently are?	1.1.1 Actual performance to your targets, with dates
Customer	Same layout as above for goals in this area.				
Business Processes	Same layout as above for goals in this area.				
Learning & Growth	Same layout as above for goals in this area.				

117

Now that you know the importance of measuring the right things the right way, have set challenging but realistic targets that are timebound, and have designed control systems that allow you to see what is going on automatically, it's time to talk about how you prove it all!

Proving it: *it's all about the data!*

The Importance of Data Quality

Having data and information is great but having high-quality data to derive your information from is even better. What do I mean by high-quality data? Data you can trust, data that has traceability, and data that has controls and security wrapped around it so that you know what you are looking at to ensure the data has not been compromised in any way.

What do I mean by compromised? Think of it this way, data should be secure once it is entered into the process and becomes part of your system of record. Whether that data was manually entered, scanned in, or derived through intelligent automation (IA), you should always be in complete control of it, meaning that you can prove that no one has altered or manipulated it in any way (think data security breaches, both external and internal).

Why is data quality so important? Because you are going to make decisions on it for yourself and your business, and if the data you are making these decisions from is not high quality, then you can imagine the negative consequences.

Two key things to understand about data quality are whether it is secure and traceable and if there is a good understanding of the data population itself. What are the demographics of the data? Does it represent a comprehensive population that is unbiased, or is it taken from a population that may already skew the results one way or another?

Let me give you a quick example here. Let's say you wanted to do a survey on what percentage of people love to swim to decide on whether to build a new pool in a town. Well, if you went to the current pool and surveyed a hundred people there (which statistically would give you a valid data size) and asked them if they loved to swim, the majority would say yes. Now, if you did not know where that survey was taken and just looked at the results of the data questions, you could draw an easy conclusion that you should go ahead and build a new pool because over 90% of your "population" says you should. But that may possibly be a wrong conclusion since the survey population was skewed, or what is called "non-valid" because of their beginning preference (everyone surveyed was already at a public pool).

So, how do you prevent making decisions from data that may not be valid? That's by always asking the question about where the original data came from (what survey or system) and then looking at how it was populated. Did you take regional sales data but are looking to make a global decision? Did you look at one product's data to make decisions on all of them? Did you survey one type of customer to make decisions for all? All things to keep in mind around the quality and understanding of your data as you look to make decisions. In the end, your data will always be what people want to discuss in order to work to invalidate it if it says something people do not like. It is your job to make sure you are absolutely confident in its quality and can prove it so you can spend time on the more important things, like what that data is saying and what you can do with that information.

The Importance of Data Access

Sometimes referred to as "findability," nothing is more frustrating than knowing you have collected the data you need for analysis and then not being able to find it. Or even worse, knowing that you collected it, knowing where it is, and then not being able to access or "get to it." Just think about how many times you have had to request access to information or data about your company to help the company run its business. Think about how wasteful that is… now what are you going to do about that?

Well, how about starting out by keeping in mind the acronym **FAIR** data, which stands for data that is (findable, accessible, interoperable, and reusable), and what I mean by that is…

- **Findable**: Data that can be located.
- **Accessible**: Data that can be located and retrieved for use.
- **Interoperable**: Data that can be used in multiple systems or applications, think standard formats.
- **Reusable**: Data sets that are accessed and used but not changed in their purest or original form.

One of the big buzzword phrases today is to "democratize the data," which means exactly what it says, data that is available to be used by the masses. It's about having sources and systems of the truth (usually multiple, controlled ones) that everyone uses to "pull" data from to make decisions. This allows everyone to be in sync with each other at the same time. This source of truth helps everyone get on the same page quicker, and thus meeting times are spent on analyzing and understanding the data and what it is telling us rather than arguing if it is true or not. This eventually enables faster decision-making and eliminates much of the organizational confusion around metrics when not having FAIR data that has trusted sources of truth.

The Importance of Data Timeliness

Ok, so we are increasing our knowledge around data and what it takes to have a good data management program. We understand how important it is to have the right data available when needed. And we learned the advantage of having data that's traceable, secure, and accessible, so what's next? Well, I would say the next thing you should be thinking about is your data timeliness because if you have everything else, yet the data is not available or updated on the schedule you need it, then it may not give you what you need to run your business. Data timeliness is unbelievably important, yet many times we settle for whatever the current timeliness is or what the systems can give us. Too often, we set the timeliness of our data reports on whatever the frequency is that the system of record will deliver it at, not when it is needed. So, a system that can only supply data quarterly will adjust everyone to manage that way, which is simply wrong since, in today's world, you more than likely need the data monthly at a minimum, and weekly is probably best. Now, in some businesses, daily data, or real-time data, may be needed too, so it really just depends on what the requirements of a business are.

How do you know if you have the right data timing for your measurement needs? Well, I recommend setting this up by how often the information should or can be looked at so that you can make process adjustments that change your output for the better. Do you want product information daily if you can only adjust your products monthly? Maybe weekly data would be better for that? Do you need customer satisfaction data daily if you only meet on it with your team monthly? You need to constantly remember to balance the work it takes to produce the data you need with the value that you actually get from that data. If your data is actionable when you get it, and allows you to do something with it, then that's great. If it doesn't give you that capability, then you should look at it to see if you really need it. Nothing is worse than you or your team collecting data for reports that are not used; this kills a good performance measurement program quicker than anything. So, live by the mantra, "What is the minimal amount of data and information I need to run my business, keep it in control, and keep me informed?" Not "Let's collect everything I can, look at hundreds of different ways, and hope there is something good in there." The best MTC processes understand that less is more. The higher the quality, the better.

The Importance of Data Visibility

Now that we have the data that we need to tell us what is going on, it's time to put it in a format that brings out the information in the data. Data "visibility" is one of the most important parts of your MTC process but often the one that gets the least attention.

Think of your data visibility as your presentation layer, where you are putting data into a format that you and others can understand. Your data's information should jump out and catch someone's attention without the need for explanation. If it does need you to explain it, then it's too complicated, which unfortunately happens with lots of data presentations. So not only is it important to think about how you want the data presented, but also how the receivers of that data, other than you, want to consume it. Do they want it in mobile format to view remotely? Do they want it available at all times of the day and night in all parts of the world? Would they like it "pushed" to them, or are they okay with getting it from an online connection? These are just some of the detailed questions you need to address in your data visibility program process.

As we mentioned in the data quality section, the first thing a high-quality MTC program has is deep knowledge and control around its data. Not only where it came from and if it's secure, which we covered, but also exactly what data you have and what its characteristics are, and then you can decide what the best way to look at it is.

This is how I recommend you look at your data:

Start out simple

Let's face it, we've all been in meetings or presentations or sent information where it is hard, and sometimes even impossible, to figure out the intent of the charts and graphs you are looking at. That's why it is so important to start out simple. Sticking to some basic pie charts and bar or line graphs. It may seem basic, but you'd be amazed at how impactful they can be when used and analyzed correctly.

Some Simple Data Display Examples

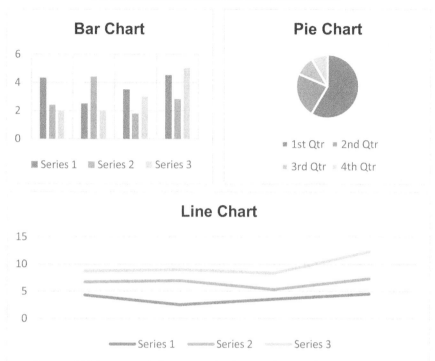

Simple visible data is easy to explain, and the analytics provided by data analysts can quickly lead to great information and, thus, solid business decisions. But before we get to that, let me explain a few small nuances about the data analysis process.

The process of data analysis usually starts in its raw form, which means it comes right out of your data collection system. Now, in a perfect world, your data collection system (these can be any of the systems you use to run your business) would allow you to look at your data any way you would like, having built-in robust analytics capabilities. But, while analytics are getting better in many systems, most of the time, this is not the case, so the data is exported to another system that has been designed for data analytics and presentation—tools like MS Excel, Tableau, Power BI, Fusion

Charts, Qlik Sense, and Domo, just to name a few. When the data is exported to this system, the tougher job begins, which is trying to understand what that data is telling us. I'm not going to dive into all the nuances around what expertise you need to really understand and analyze your data, but let's suffice it to say that having data scientists and data analysts are worth their weight in gold here.

So, now that you have a little deeper understanding of how the data has gotten to the point of being ready for visibility and presentation. And you have seen some of the simple charts that can be used to display it. Let's move on to more complex ways to present the data and see how that allows a deeper and more informed understanding of what that data is saying.

Adding more complexity to your visualization

By taking the simple two-variable bar chart I showed above and adding a third variable to it, you have just increased the data on it by 50% and hopefully the information on it too. This is a simple step to increasing your visualization's usefulness without overdoing it.

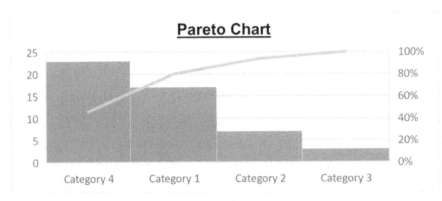

Pareto Chart

* By the way, the Pareto chart is where the term 80/20 rule comes from, meaning 80% of your issues comes from 20% of your categories.

Before we continue, I would like to explain two keywords that I briefly mentioned before that are often used incorrectly in the field of data analytics. They are *correlation* and *causality*, and their simple definitions are…

Correlation: A mutual relationship or connection between two or more things. Interdependence of variable quantities. Ex: cold weather may be the reason people bought more jackets.

Causality: The relationship between cause and effect. The principle that everything has a cause. Ex: temperatures below 32° F will cause water to turn to ice.

As you can see from these definitions, these are two similar but different words. The reason I bring them up at this point is that as you expand the data that you are trying to represent in visualizations, it's always good to see if you can show how the data is correlated or caused (causality). If you can show this in some way, people will tend to remember it longer; thus, the information in your data will be that much more valuable.

So, please use these words correctly and visibly in your information display. You'll be glad you did!

Data Visibility, what to watch out for…

- **Too much data, or too complex a representation**

Simply put, if it must be explained to someone in your industry, line of work, level of responsibility, or company, then it is too complex. What I mean by this is that graphs, charts, and other ways to make information visible and understandable are only effective if they can be understood by the end user. Now, if that is you, and you are not going to share the information with more than a very small group of highly-trained or educated experts, then having to explain it might be okay. But the usual process is someone not as qualified as the person that made the data visible (the designer) is going to have to use it, and without the designer around, it becomes impossible to understand and very frustrating indeed!

- **Too narrow a view of your data**

With too narrow a view of data, you run the risk of not seeing the complete picture and interpreting it incorrectly. When data does not have a wide enough window, you may worry about a problem that you don't really have, like looking at one bad week of sales and reacting to it, when what you didn't see was that the preceding two weeks and following two weeks were just fine and made up for the bad week. Too small a window usually causes extra work in a company, so be aware of that.

- **Too wide a view of your data**

When you look too widely at a data set, you run the risk of losing the details in the information. Looking at a year's worth of data, or even a quarter's worth, may not give you the information to see things you need to see to fix them, like seasonality, impulse issues caused by events outside your control, et cetera.

- **Not having directional information on your data**

Having a too narrow or too wide a view of your data is a problem. But the real question is if you have a relative view of it. What this means is how it's compared to something. How does your data look the same time last year? Is it up or down, and what direction is it moving in? Is it tracking the same as last year, month, or quarter? Without this information, you again may make erroneous decisions due to incomplete data, so be aware of that.

Averages... and the "flaw" of them

The term "average," also mistakenly referred to as the mean, is defined as a number expressing the typical central value in a data set. Average is calculated by dividing the sum of the values in the set by their total number *(Average=Sum of all the values / Total number of values)*. You probably hear this term daily, whether it is describing some type of experience, "our meal was just average," or a certain data set, "the average return on my investments is XX%," yet we sometimes forget that while it is a great descriptor for the typical value, it may not be the best one for the outcome of something that touches your customer and to run your business on. Simply put, this term can give you a false sense of good performance and needs to be applied sparingly; let me explain.

Say your customer guarantee is to deliver your product to them in five days, and you are looking to do that 90% of the time since you know there will be times you can't meet that commitment. Now, if you set up your target in your measurement system trying to achieve a 90% average and you just use the equation for averages above, the issue is this. Say you have a hundred shipments in a week, and fifty of them arrive in three days, which is great. But the other fifty arrive in six days, which is not so good. Well, if you apply the average equation from above on these results, your average would be 4.5 days, which would mean you would report 100% on-time delivery to your target of five days, which would give you a false sense of security.

The better way to measure performance for this would be to use the % at a certain level, which is five days. This tells you that 50% of your deliveries arrived within five days and 50% took more than five days. This is a more accurate view of what is going on. So instead of an inaccurate 4.5-day average delivery time, you have accurate data that reveals that 50% of your shipments are late. Now you know where you need to improve in your delivery process.

Also, be careful when using averages for large data sets, even when all you are looking for is the average. Variations in your outcomes are what customers feel the most and make them wary about your overall performance. If you have a delivery time target of five days, and your performance is somewhere in the one-to-five-day range, with an occasional six, then your average can easily be your five days. But the inconsistency of delivery across those five days is what the customer feels because they have no idea what day their delivery will arrive in that five-day span. So, keep in mind it is not only the average you should measure but the deviation from that average, which will give you much better information to act on.

Data Analytics: *it's what you do with all that data that really matters*

So, as we get ready to close out this chapter, I'd like to talk about something that is paramount to the success of a well-designed MTC program. And that is first understanding what data analytics is and then understanding what the roles are that make it all happen.

Data management is the complete process of inspecting, cleansing, transforming, and modeling data with the goal of discovering useful information or conclusions from that analysis. Data analytics is more about the final process steps here, examining the collected data sets to find trends and draw conclusions about the information. Increasingly, data analytics is done with the aid of specialized systems and software due to data size and equation complexity.

In order to make data analytics happen, there is usually a team of people focused on it. Data architects, data engineers, data scientists, and data analysts are the roles that are usually applied here. They are the people that will make "magic" happen with your data. I know, sounds like a lot of people to "do data," but in today's world, split-second decisions are needed to run many businesses. The amount of data available in the world is doubling less than every two years right now because of the digitization of everything. It is important to make sure you have this work defined, understood, and have these qualified people; otherwise, you may miss one of these very important pieces. What are they, you ask? Well, their definitions are...

- **Data Scientist:** A data professional with strong business and technological skills who uses advanced tools, modeling, and algorithms to perform assessments on data.

- **Data Architect:** Data technology professional who works in data management and designs the architect and frameworks of the data, which helps companies organize, retrieve, interpret, store, maintain and share data.

- **Data Engineer:** Data technology professional who helps organizations analyze data by creating algorithms to find trends in the data and translate the data for operational uses. Helps other employees in an organization access and interpret raw data and often build the infrastructure to manage the data architect designs.

- **Data Analyst:** Data professional who gathers and interprets data to solve problems and identify trends. Often responsible for creating reports, charts, or graphics that help others understand the information they find in their data sets.

Why do we need each? Well, that's easy. Look deeply into those definitions and understand that each of these roles produces different outcomes that are needed by the others. Thus, you can have them as separate roles, or if you are a small company, they can be combined, but the defined pieces of work still need to be accomplished. Their teamwork in collecting, organizing, managing, and sharing data is what it is all about.

Also, these roles are what set up and focus your data analytics program. Doing so usually moves your focus from referring solely to last month's sales reports to predictive and intelligent analytics. Switching from discussing what has happened to what may happen and how to prevent something from happening, or better yet, how to make something happen!

Overall, we covered a lot of very important material in this chapter. But there are a few important things to keep in mind. A great MTC program is about keeping your mind on your targeted outcome by not having too many measures of success, by not being satisfied until you get to where you have planned to go, and also by taking the time to look behind you to see what you have achieved. It allows you to reflect on your journey so far and celebrate that, and then move on to the next challenge!

To achieve *Better Outcomes:*

- **Metrics,** are they SMART?
- **Targets,** how will you know when you have achieved them?
- **Controls,** are yours the right ones in the right places?
- Is your data "visualized" and available for all to use?
- A small amount of great data and graphics trumps too much data every time. What does yours look like?

Is your MTC program set up to make you successful by measuring the right things right?

... think about it.

Chapter 7

Innovation and Creativity
... why are they so important?

*"In the beginner's mind there are many possibilities...
in the expert's mind there are few."*

–Erik Wahl, Unthink

Why is Innovation so important?

Because, if done correctly, innovation keeps you ahead of your competition. It's also the lifeblood of business and personal success. How many times have you heard people say, "If we stay still, we will get run over," or "We have to keep moving forward, or we will die."? (That last one is kind of dramatic.) Perhaps you have even said, "I wish I came up with that idea."

No matter the statement, everyone understands the significance of innovation. Whether you're a company of one or employ a team of thousands, the only way to remain competitive is to harness your innovative thinking and the creative outcomes of that thinking.

However, there's a problem with today's innovation. Most companies think that innovation should be limited to one department, like research and design (R&D), and rely on that department as their innovation engine. It's true that departments like R&D are necessary for the development of complex new products— cancer drugs and new airplanes come to mind. What's also true is that innovation is not confined to R&D alone. It's not just product innovation that's critical; service innovation, financial innovation, communication innovation, and even leadership innovation are all integral. Innovation is about continuous reinvention. To stay ahead of the competition, continuous reinvention should be part of everything you do.

Everyone on your team is responsible for innovative and creative thinking. Your team should always be thinking ahead about how they can do their job better tomorrow.

There is no limit on when or from where innovation and creative thinking can originate. Innovation comes from pondering, "What could be?" It comes from looking at the world around you and using your mind to play out the question of "What if?" *What if I did it this way? What if I changed or added this, or removed that?* The possibilities are infinite, and they all begin with thinking differently.

Let's look at the quotation from the beginning of the chapter: *"In the beginner's mind, there are many possibilities; in the expert's mind, there are few."* I believe that the lack of possibilities in the mind of the expert is the root cause of our current creative thinking deficit. I also believe this can and will change, and we will become a more innovative society. Nevertheless, it will take time.

Think about it. How many times have you been at a meeting or social event where you have brought up a new idea, only to have someone tell you why it won't work or isn't possible? Typically, that person will justify their position by claiming they have experience. They state that their experience is how they know the idea won't work. Ever notice how that experience is in the past. I love to think about how much innovation and discovery scientists, explorers, and others have accomplished because they decided to go against conventional wisdom or against whatever their past experience has told them. They decided to strike out on their own to get something done, or at least try!

A great example of this is the advent of PCs in the early eighties. Many of the early PC pioneers—IBM, Compaq, Wang—went forward even when the industry told them that no one would ever need a computer at home. They claimed that computers would only be good as a typewriter replacement and that they were way too expensive for the average consumer to afford. What they missed was not where the technology was at that time. Instead, they lacked the vision to see where it would eventually go. Soon, Apple came in with a graphical interface, along with CDs for video on the PC, and the rest is history.

The world is full of "experts" who like to talk about why something won't work or can't be done because it's easier to do that than to figure out how to get it done. The real work, and the people we remember the most, are not the people who said it couldn't be done (we call them the naysayers). We remember the people that did get it done. The ones we like to refer to as the pioneers. Think about it. Where would we be today without the Wright Brothers (airplanes), John Roebling (Brooklyn Bridge), or Henry Ford (mass production)? How about some lesser-known but still important pioneers like Fairchild Semiconductor, Intel's PC microprocessors, and Apple's graphical interfaces? All of these are examples of people or companies that were told something couldn't be done. Fortunately, they disregarded the "experts" and went out and proved them wrong.

Why do people, and some companies, fail or forget to innovate?

Besides what I just mentioned about having those naysayers, a lot of companies are still rooted in the thinking that innovation is some department's job rather than everyone's, although this is slowly shifting. Along with this thinking, another major impediment to innovation is company cultures rooted too much in their past traditions. I've seen and personally been part of cultures that put more of a premium on doing great meeting presentations and having great slides than having innovative content in those slides, mainly because of their aversion to risk-taking. This is the one thing that kills innovation the quickest and one that risk-averse companies thrive on. The more presentations there are on a certain risk, the more people are usually involved in the final decision. That leaves the decisions to a committee and not just one or a few. Thus, innovation either gets stalled or eliminated because true innovators want to move fast and do not have all the answers that risk-averse executives want. In the end, these "presentations" cause so much friction that your creative people leave for more innovative companies, which usually means smaller, more nimble ones.

Why is it smaller companies are more innovative, you say. Just think, fewer levels of management mean fewer levels that have to approve things, and without the budget of a huge company to buy them time, they need to work quicker. Smaller companies are part of a faster-moving culture because they have faster-moving competitors fighting for that creative edge every day.

I want to mention one final note on something that stymies innovation in companies: the "not-invented-here syndrome." This describes behavior where innovation generated outside the immediate team (or silo in a large company) is looked at as foreign and is resisted because of its origin, not because of its merit. This is very detrimental in larger companies and causes a lot of excess spending because of not borrowing from ideas or lessons already learned. Nothing is worse for employee morale and a company's bottom line than reinventing the wheel repeatedly just because an idea didn't originate in the area or silo you work in, yet it happens often.

So, with all these headwinds going against innovation, why should you be optimistic that this will ever get better? Well, that's because the progress in digital information (think internet) has opened everyone up to be able to expand their knowledge in so many different areas. This allows more people to see what could be, to see others are doing things, to see where things can be improved, or new markets can be created, and thus personal innovation over the past years has really accelerated. Think about how many new products from vendors you never heard of are on e-commerce sites like Amazon, Etsy, Wayfarer, Walmart, Target, et cetera. So many of these are new and innovative products that were able to be brought to market because of new and innovative retail channels and digital capabilities.

Spurring Innovation

Innovation can come from anyone, anywhere, at any time… but the origins that spur innovation come from having true purpose, open thinking, creative dialogues, a future focus on what could be, and a true culture of risk-taking. It breeds best in an environment rich in knowledge and lacking in fear that unleashes our imagination!

> *"Everything you can imagine is real."*
> *–P. Picasso*

Innovation is not something you "go out and do." It is more something that you create an environment for, so it can happen. Many of today's leaders/managers think that if you free up people's time at work, then they will use that time to innovate, which I have found not to be always true; you must create opportunities and slight direction for them. You must because if you really think about it, we constantly look to hire or grow the best and brightest people, but that also gives us people that think, or have learned, about things in a certain structured way. Thus, the importance of bringing in new people and ways of thinking, and challenging certain established ways of thinking, or norms as we like to call them, at all times is extremely important, and must be constantly encouraged.

One of the best things you can do as a leader and a manager is to create a climate of innovation. In their book, *Head, Heart, and Guts: How the World's Best Companies Develop Complete Leaders,* Stephen Rhinesmith, David Dotlich, and Peter Cairo talk about the climate needed for innovation to flourish and six main thoughts to focus on in your environment to make it happen. Over the years, these thoughts/guidelines have always stuck with me, and they are…

- Outside-in perspective… what is the need?
- Clarity of purpose or problem statement.
- Idea generation and research.
- Idea support from within and above.
- Execution and measurement.
- Recognition, pass or fail, and then repeat!

One thing to keep in mind here is the seven-step scientific method that we discussed in our earlier chapters. You can see the similarities between them here, with the importance of clarity in your problem statement, research, ideation, execution, and measurement. All great discovery and innovation processes continue to have their basis in this.

Another thought to keep in mind here is the importance of agile thinking and agile execution in an innovative environment. Subtle processes or procedures that slow down or interfere with the innovative process (remember, it can happen at any time, so your environment must always be ready for it). Let me tell you a quick story about this.

Many years ago, back when I was an engineer at Hewlett-Packard, I was working late one night in our facility on Page Mill Road in Palo Alto when I heard a commotion back in our technical parts storage area, so I went to see what was going on. What I saw was Bill Hewlett with a bolt cutter in his hands, cutting a lock that was on our technical parts storage area. When I inquired about what was going on, I was told that Bill had just dropped by to say hello (he loved to "hang out" with the engineers; he was one himself) and heard that the team had become frustrated by a new rule that locked the parts cage because too many parts were being used for experiments. Now, you had to sign the parts out and have a key to access them. Well, this did not sit well with Bill, to say the least. It had never been this way before, and let's just say after the lock-cutting incident, the new rule was changed, and the parts were freely accessed again. Why did Bill want this area always accessible?

Because he understood that innovation happens at all hours of the day and night, and locking something up that people needed to innovate (back then, you would grab parts and just start building things for fun on something called a "breadboard") would inhibit innovation. He also realized that if someone was worried that we were using too many parts, then the issue was to find out why that was, not just stifle all of it, and if they needed more funding for extra parts so people could be creative, then as a $16B company at the time someone should just ask.

What I saw that day stayed with me as a forever leadership lesson and as a lesson in innovation, and I still laugh when I think about it.

In *Unthink: How to Rediscover Your Creative Genius*, Erik Wahl discusses why we are not good at being innovative but then also points out how we can learn to be good at it. He discusses how at an early age, we were inquisitive and questioned everything, and eventually, that curiosity was dampened down by statements from people we respected: *It's always been done that way, now stop asking*, or *Because I said so*. Think of how early in life you started to hear that and how you still hear it today. So, what did we learn from that? *We learned to stop asking questions at an early age* because it makes people feel uncomfortable, and that's where we are today. We accept rather than question, and when we do question, we accept the answers from people in authority, whether we agree with the answer or not, rarely questioning the answers. We lost the awe, and engine, of our imagination, which was to ponder the why's!

Now think about this. How about every time you asked a question, you were sat down and explained exactly what the answers meant, why it was a good question, and encouraged to continue to ask questions. When was the last time you really heard that? Think about the power of that… and think about how the democratization of data and information due to the internet, social media, and things like IA (intelligent automation) and AI (artificial intelligence) have made it possible for everyone to get answers to most of their questions literally at their fingertips (we Google things every day, right?). The power that these new capabilities are now unleashing is just being realized, and that is why I'm so optimistic that society's creativity will only expand going forward.

In *Unthink*, Erik also points out some keywords (with excellent descriptions and expansion) to remember for the future and to learn or recapture your creativity, ones that I think you should all keep in mind to increase or grow your own and your team's innovation; they are:

- Be Provocative
- Be Intuitive
- Be Convicted
- Be Accelerated
- Be Spontaneous
- … and Be Original, **you are the only you!**

The final thought I have for you around innovation and creativity is to remember that anyone can do it and become good at it, but it does take a little work. To become good at asking "What if?" you need to know what *could be*. To know what *could be* means you have to keep up with a lot of things happening in multiple industries. You must resist the urge to have someone else come in and "be your expert" and spend the time becoming more informed. It is one thing to ask others to be creative for you or your company because you value their outside perspective and outside view of the world. It is totally another to have someone else do this for you because you say you don't have the time for it or are not good at it. All that says is innovation and creativity are not that important to you, and your success, which I would truly doubt is what you are really looking to say in today's competitive business environment.

To achieve *Better Outcomes:*

- Are you thinking **"What if?"** and **"What could be?"** everyday?
- Are you spending time figuring out how to get it done rather than why it can't be done?
- Do you operate with a not-invented-here mentality or are you open to ideas from everywhere?
- Are you continuing to ask "why?" until you get the real root cause answer?
- Are you moving your innovative and creative thinking fast enough to overcome the inertia resisting it?

Are you going to operate with an expert's skepticism or with a beginner's awe and creativity?

... think about it.

Chapter 8

The Process of Management
... *both science and art!*

"Most of what we call management consists of making it difficult for people to get their work done."

–Peter Drucker

Managers, oh my God, how we love to hate them, and yet, many times, we strive to be one. Why is that? Well, for the first statement, "we love to hate them," I have found that the main reason is because of what we hear about them from others or experience ourselves, and that is usually negative. Why is that? Many times, the main reason for this is because negative or bad news travels ten times faster, with twice the frequency and distance than good news (if you don't believe that, just look at your local news shows or on social media). Thus, unfortunately, we hear all about examples of bad management and very little about good management. I want to be clear on something right now, management is not a bad word, and it is very needed in organizations. There are many examples of good management at many companies—we just don't talk about that as much due to the tendencies of human nature, as mentioned above. So, knowing this, what we are going to spend our time on here is the process to become a great manager, why that's important, and how to go about doing just that. Starting with what I call the process of management, or POM.

Now, before we get started on the process of management and how to be good at it, I wanted to quickly explain the difference between management and leadership (which we discuss much deeper in **Part III** of the book), so here we go...

- **Management:** The conducting or supervising of something; a distinct process consisting of *planning, organizing, actuating,* and *controlling* to accomplish predetermined objectives. It is referred to as a *science* because of the standardization of many of these processes, and the ease of their repeatability across businesses globally.
- **Leadership:** Encompasses the ability of an individual, group, or organization to "lead," influence, or guide other individuals or organizations. The word "leadership" has varied definitions. It is a "contested" term that literature and research often debate because of the different viewpoints and contrasting approaches to leadership taken around the world, in different countries and cultures. This is why it is referred to as an *art,* because it is viewed and felt differently by each individual person.

As you can see from these "definitions," and I say that loosely because there are many deviations of these definitions, the best way to think of these two terms are: **Management is more of a science and is about the "What and How." Leadership is more of an art form and is about the "Why."** This is why the word "management" is defined more precisely, and debated less, than the word "leadership". This is also why we can and will look at the process of management, which will allow us to look deeper into the individual pieces of a well-defined management process and learn from them.

As noted above, our management definition says it is a well-defined process with four distinct parts. While I do agree with that, I have always added a few more parts so that the pieces fit together into a management "flow," and thus, we get this *seven-step process of management.*

The 7-Step Process of Management (POM)

The Process of Management

Plan and Re-Plan

Start here, for yourself, your business, and your career, both short and long-term, because *if you fail to plan, then plan to fail*. If you did everything correctly in **Part I** of the book, then you should be all set here. Just remember, though, that the conditions you planned for, and the data you planned with, are all dynamic (constantly changing). This constant change is why it's important to continuously monitor those original assumptions and replan by adjusting your ASA, SWOT, strategic plan, and measures of success when necessary.

Hire and Organize

Nothing is more important than getting the right people into the right jobs at the right time and place to help you deliver your strategy because, with the right people, strategy, and execution, all forms of challenges and opportunities can be solved. In *Execution: The*

Discipline of Getting Things Done, Larry Bossidy and Ram Charan talk about the shortcomings of the traditional people process, which is backward-looking, focused on hiring and evaluating people for the jobs being done today rather than tomorrow, and it's a thought I have always remembered. It is so easy to get pulled into solving the problem right in front of us, which, although important, it is equally as important to be anticipating what is coming next and be prepared for that, and that all starts with the right people and their right capabilities.

I say hire for a person's DNA (characteristics and capabilities) and fit to your culture, not narrowly focused job requirements. You can use them as a guide to what you are looking for, but with the ever-changing dynamics of all customers and industries, if you hire for too narrow of a job description, you run the risk of your people not being able to adjust to these changing requirements. Many job requirements are written too narrowly around certain skills they are looking for rather than the characteristics of people. Keep in mind that skills can be taught, but characteristics are much harder to change.

Some other things to consider as you hire and organize your team…

- **Recruiting…** Where and when does it start? Well, what I like to say is that when you have a business where you have employees, then recruiting is a constant. You should always be on the lookout for great talent with the DNA you are looking for because you just never know where you are going to find them. I have made some of my best hires over the years from people I have met working in restaurants (great customer service people), traveling, the local gym, et cetera. Always be aware of what talent you need and where and when you need it so you can continuously be on the lookout for it! Don't kid yourself. There is a war for talent out there, and there always has been for great people, so always keep that in mind and always be recruiting.

- **Onboarding...** A good or bad new employee relationship deserves a positive experience right from the start, and your onboarding process can make or break this. This process should start immediately from the point of job acceptance. The employee should be made to feel like they have joined a great company and team that is extremely glad they have decided to bring their talent to them and can't wait for them to start. It should not wait for the employee to show up on day one to begin the onboarding process. Although that is an important date, it should start before that with welcoming packages sent to their home that give them information on their new employer, their teammates, and the new culture, and can even include their new work tools like cell phones and PCs. The direct hiring manager should reach out to thank them for joining and let them know what to expect on the first day and week. So much opportunity to get this right from the start, yet many times it's overlooked.
  - **The 90-day experience for new hires.** The first ninety days can make or break a new hire's success and longevity. As important as the pre-arrival is before the first day, the next ninety days are even more important. Make sure the new hire has a mentor-friend-helper for those first ninety days. Someone to help them navigate the new environment and to help decode the company acronyms and culture goes a long way in helping retain your employees later.

- **Designing and operationalizing the organization...** Even if you recruit, hire, and onboard correctly, one of the main things a manager must now do is to arrange those resources correctly to get the optimum outcome. It all starts with enabling the process of getting something done, not disabling it, so the placement of your new hires into a well-designed organizational structure is paramount.

Your organization's design or structure should root itself in enabling your processes to flow by helping your employees operate the process. If designed correctly, there should be a minimal amount of managerial overhead, just enough to give the employees what they need to do their job, to observe and coach them where needed, and not add any managerial burden (like reports, non-value-added meetings, etc.) to the process. If done correctly, a good organizational design increases accountability, speed of decision-making, and overall morale and performance. One last thing about organizational structure—it should be designed from the work, or bottom, up, not from the leadership down, which, when done correctly, will help you have the right number of managerial layers, spans, and controls to make work flow and get the job done!

- **Diversity and Inclusion...** These are not just the buzzwords of today, they are two words that have always been extremely important, and they are very different. Diversity is about having an employee population that mirrors the society you operate in, wherever it is in the world. It is about having people that come from different backgrounds, religions, regions, ethnicity, sexual preference, ages, gender, etc., so you can have diversity of thought that eventually leads you to great ideas, directions, and decisions. Diversity starts with your hiring process and needs to become part of your active DNA in hiring, not an add-on after the fact. Inclusion is ensuring you involve employees' different thoughts, points of view, and past experiences in and out of work, in your decisions and ensure you actively solicit, understand, and use them as much as possible.

- **Keeping the right people...** I hate to do it, but I must mention this because it is so important to your success. We must admit that we are not all perfect, and thus, occasionally, we will make a mistake in our hiring process and choose the wrong person to join our team. The first thing to do is to understand that when this happens, this is a failure of management and the hiring process, not the candidate's fault (unless there was some misrepresentation on their part). This needs to be addressed in an understanding and empathetic way as soon as possible because avoidance of the wrong hire is not good for all parties involved. The sooner you correct your mistake, figure out how it happened, and learn from that to try to prevent it from happening again in the future, the better it will be for all. Avoiding a "wrong hire" in hopes that they will quit is not addressing it—it's avoiding your responsibility as a leader.

Develop your Team and Yourself

Education, I think you will all agree, is so important to our success as a society and the world in general, so why is it that as soon as companies start to miss their financial targets, it's one of the first budget items to get cut? Think about it, have you ever worked somewhere you have been told there is no money for training, continuing education assistance, online seminars, etc., because sales or profits are down? How much sense does that make?

My view on training and continuous learning for yourself and your company is this: if you think learning and knowledge are too expensive to fund, then you should try ignorance for a while and see how that works out for you and your business. In the process of management, hiring and keeping great people is Job #1, but then helping them to learn and grow is Job #1A because the deeper and faster your people develop, the more they can contribute to the outcomes of your business and the better it is for all.

In today's world, with the speed that business is moving, it is imperative you keep yourself and your employees up to speed on the latest education and knowledge they need to do their jobs and coach them accordingly. It's one thing to tell people to become smarter; it's another thing to help them along the way with suggestions, examples, and ongoing coaching. Here are a few things to keep in mind in this very important area:

- **Targeted and Timely training...** In your overall strategic plan's HR plan, you should have training plans by roles, levels, and locations. Some roles need more training than others, simply because that specialty may be changing faster in the industry, like product development and technology. Some others may not need as much, but all need some. It is up to you to think about it at the beginning of each year, and the best place to find out about your training needs is to ask the people who are doing the work. You'll be amazed at how much they know about what they need. Oh, and don't forget about the ever-important soft-skills training, since those are even more important than deep technical and business knowledge training in many cases. The world is full of intelligent people that can't get their point across because they failed to develop their presentation and listening skills.

- **Develop before needed…** Sounds simple, right? Well, I can't tell you how many times I have looked to fund training for someone on my team only to find out that since the person wasn't in the position that the knowledge would be used in yet, our corporate policy wouldn't fund it. How are employees to train for new or expanded roles? Talk about a poor policy. The time to get someone the training they will need for their next role is before they get it; otherwise, you risk the person getting into the role and not being successful. Common sense, right?

- **Coaching…** It's one of the most important techniques for developing people, yet the skill set is often overlooked. Coaching is about letting people know when they are doing a good job and why that is, as much as it is about pointing out when they are not. It's about walking people through their roles and work when they first get started and then observing and helping them along the way as they "play the game." Coaching is about guiding people to the win, not telling them how to do it and then sitting by idly and letting them know monthly or weekly how they are doing. It is one of the most needed managerial skills in the industry, and while it is also about leadership, it really is just a basic management principle. If you are in any managerial position and have never had any formal training on how to be a good coach, then I recommend you proactively go get some. The return on your investment is huge here, and your people will thank you for it. The biggest thing about a great coach (I'm sure you can all remember one from your past) is that they are teachers and guides, not directors.

- **Promotions...** Promote for company need, not because someone has had a title or been in a position for a long time. The best promotions are the ones where someone has done such a great job that either their role has grown because of their good work or a role at the next level up has opened, and they are the most qualified candidate. If this is the case and you handle it correctly, everyone will feel good about the promotion. Promoting people because they have just been in a role a long time or because you are afraid they will leave is never a good idea and will cause other issues in the long run. Better to give someone a bonus for doing a great job in their current role than to create the future problem of having more high-level people than needed, which will come back to haunt you.

One last recommendation, I always set a goal for each employee for training hours they need to formally accomplish each year, and then give them time to do it. Many professionals, like teachers, lawyers, doctors, etc., must do this to stay accredited. Nothing's as insincere as giving your people, or yourself, a goal of developing themselves but then not setting aside time for them to be able to do it. I promise you will get the return in productivity over the years that you lose to the hours spent in the training.

Actuate

Okay, we hired, we organized, we trained, and we are ready to coach, so now let's go! I say the only thing left before we push the "start" button is to make sure everyone understands where they fit in the process to deliver so they understand what the importance of their contributions is to the outcome. Lots of times, people have difficulty understanding how what they do is valuable to the paying customer or business, and you need to explain that and help them understand their value. If you can't, then that is a different issue. Actuation is often combined with run and control, but I have found that to be successful in that step, you need to start things off correctly. Some thoughts on actuating:

- **Communicate the *whys*...** One more time! Make sure everyone understands the intended outcomes.

- **Open channels of communication...** Have them up and down the organization so there is a two-way dialogue the minute something happens outside of the plan or if someone needs help.

- **Communicate honestly, timely, and directly...** Make sure managers/leaders up and down the organizational chain and across boundaries are **communicating directly** with vision, passion, and realistic optimism. Everyone should understand the strategic direction and plans for full engagement, even people out of your area or silo, so they can help if needed.

- **Apply leadership (honesty, integrity, empathy, and active listening...** Remember why you hired that diverse team. Make sure you engage people's hearts and minds and that at the end of the day, people will forget what you have said to them or what they have accomplished, **but they will never forget how you made them feel,** so make them feel great always (something I wish I'd learned earlier in my career). Having and using empathy is key here.

Run and Control

Here we are! We are finally in our day-to-day work, or should I say battles. Think of run and control as what we do every day. It is what we lead and accomplish on an ongoing basis and is usually what we are most proud of. In the managerial world, this is what you are responsible for delivering and what all your strategic preparation has led you to. So, what do you do every day to make sure you are moving this forward and driving this well? Let's think about these things…

- **Metrics, targets, and controls:** Are we delivering on what our plan was, and are we meeting our targets and commitments, either to ourselves or to our company and even our employees? The importance of feedback loops in your process cannot be overstated. It's the glue for strategic connection and accountability. Can you automate it?

- **Provide connected feedback and coaching:** Are you keeping your employees up to date on how they are doing their specific work and how the total work outcome is coming out? Too often, we just let them know how they did on their piece of the work, which is important, but they also need to know how the customer outcome came out and what the customer thought, if possible. Helps them improve their own work processes if needed.

- **Real-time procedure performance visibility:** This capability allows people to see how they are doing themselves; this way, they don't have to wait for you to tell them, and they can adjust things quicker.

- **Catch people doing their job right:** Avoid the habit of telling people what they are doing wrong only. Otherwise, in the long term, this will create people that know what not to do but don't know what to do. Tell them what they are doing right, with examples, and how they are doing it right, with details, so they can repeat that behavior!

- **Multi-skill your people:** Make sure people are aware not only of their role but what is going on directly to the left and right of their role, sometimes referred to as "upstream" and "downstream," in case something is not happening, and they must help.

- **Process and people servant:** Be an enabler, take away roadblocks. Ask and see what people need to get their job done, not what you need to do yours, and get it for them. Be an exceptional manager and be the reason people want to come back to work tomorrow and do it again!

Learn and Adjust

You should always "actively manage" your business regardless of if it is yours or someone else's. Constantly loop back and see if you have the visibility and controls to adjust things as they go and if that information is available for others to use, that they are using it. I have seen many examples over the years of great control metrics that were put in place that no one really used, usually because people don't trust the data anymore, or never did, so the systems become less responsive to that data over the years. Learn from your feedback data and adjust your plans and processes according to what it tells. Some tips for adjustment are...

- **Analyze the data and then adjust:** Your data may tell you that you must make some hard decisions; **do it!** You may have to ruthlessly re-prioritize work/orders to the resource levels or capabilities you have available to meet commitments; **do it!** You may have to adjust your product mix, selling more of the profitable ones and less of the not-so-profitable ones; **do it!** You may even have to adjust your complete strategic plan because of unforeseen changes in the macro environment; **do it!** I can't stress the importance of trusting and using your data to make timely changes, and the keyword here is *timely*.

- **Resist the urge:** Don't jump on the first data you see or the data that's RED. Data gives you the first point that something is going on, not a definitive one, so learn to interpret your data with a skeptic's eye, be it GREEN, YELLOW, or RED, and try to understand it deeply before making any changes.

- **Adjustment frequency:** Adjust as needed if it is to fix the root cause of an issue or capitalize on something new. Keep in mind that many companies only adjust after quarterly info and thus only get three times a year to impact an entire year, not exactly responsive to the data. Adjustments are like metrics and should be planned accordingly. Just resist the urge to set up your adjustments to the timeliness of the data because this may be too fast or slow. Your culture has a lot to do with this since it may introduce lots of changes in your processes and procedures. While it is good to adjust to the information from the data, it's not as good to adjust all the time because you have incomplete data or you are adjusting to a symptom of an issue and not the root cause. This will wear your team out. I will talk more about this in the leadership section coming up.

- **Learn from your adjustments:** Relook at the results from your adjustments. Did they move in the direction you thought they would? Are they moving you toward your end targets? If yes, then that's good; if not, then be prepared to adjust again as you analyze more of your data.

Recognize and Reward

Recognize and reward people for doing great things in the process on an ongoing basis, not just at the end of the year. We tend to focus on rewarding the final outcomes, but what is more impactful, if possible, is to recognize and reward people as you go along. Some simple thoughts here...

- **Catch people doing things right**: Recognize and reward them for that, be specific.
- **Recognition need not be expensive:** A simple thank you in front of everyone goes a long way, although cash is nice too, and personalized gifts are the best!
- **Recognize and reward in public**: But reprimand or correct in private.

- **Call out measurable achievements:** Try to resist the urge to reward just for playing unless it's unavoidable because it is a very long project, and you need to recognize people to keep them motivated and focused.

A note on Financial Acumen

You may have noted that this is not a separate managerial step in the process of management, and that's because it is pervasive in all of them and is essential to your success. Finance and accounting are the operations that keep companies running and are the key operational processes for measures and reporting of a company, big or small, public or private. Think of finance as the team or operation that gets you the money (capital) to get you running and accounting as the way you track it all to make sure you have it under control.

The process of accounting is the one that you use for your income statement, which is the tracking mechanism that shows you your revenues, cost of goods sold (to produce), sales and general admin expenses (SG&A), and other things like depreciation. In the end, it is the document you use to see if you are running your business correctly. Underneath the income statement are the sub-processes that track your orders by customers, sales by products, and expenses by areas like production, shipping, consultants, et cetera. The things to keep in mind here are the following...

- **Income = Revenues − Expenses...** So just like your checkbook or checking account, the more you put on the positive side of your ledger, the more you can take out, and if you take out more than you put in, that's a problem. So, if your business plan shows that you are going to spend more than you are going to sell, then you need to adjust that plan or know the reason why and plan for it if you are okay with it happening.

- **Keep it simple and traceable...** Try to keep your financial accounting as streamlined as possible. The more complex this gets, the harder it is to see where you have problems. Companies get in trouble because they lose control of their finances one dollar at a time and then slowly bleed money. You may read about the big implosions of companies, but it's these smaller losses that are many times the issue.

- **Treat all monetary decisions like it was your own money...** Which it may be in a small company. Capital spending decisions should be made from the return-on-investment (ROI) angle, just like you do when you invest your own money, not from how much money your budget says you have or how much the company has available.

- **Zero-based budgeting...** Easy to say but hard to do. In an ideal business environment, each year, you should figure out exactly what you need to run the business, with a strategic and business plan that shows exactly why you are going to spend what you are asking for and what the return on that spend is going to be. But in larger companies, that is just not the case. Most of the time, each area will look at what they spent the previous year and then be asked to keep their budget flat, or with a minimal tweak up or down, for the next year. Unfortunately, this tends to underfund possible high-return investments and overfund lower-returning ones. The best way to go is to do your budgeting from the bottom up, thinking like a brand-new company every year, accounting for every dollar needed to fund your area of the business. If companies did this every year, it would be amazing how much better they would be run, and with more and more data being digital, they are getting closer to this every year.

- **Financial Education for all...** Every employee in your company should know how to read an income statement and a balance sheet. Just imagine if they could do this, how much better their decision-making could be if they thought about every dollar they spent and how it was going to affect the bottom line. Companies talk about having their employees behave more like owners, giving them more operational data than ever before to do it, but what they fail to do is give them the basic financial training they could use to help complete that request and make it all happen!

So, there's the process of management in its simplest and easiest-to-understand form (yeah, right). And just to reiterate the importance of management and its associated leadership, some recent data bears it all out. In December of 2021, GoodHire surveyed three thousand American workers, and they found that 82% of them said they would potentially quit their job because of a bad manager, the number one rated reason in their survey. Need I say more?

Now onto the 3Ps!

<u>To achieve *Better Outcomes*:</u>

- How well do you know the science of management?
- Are you **applying all seven steps in the process of management?**
  - *Plan and Replan, Hire and Organize, Develop Team and Self, Actuate, Run and Control, Learn and Adjust, and Recognize and Reward.*
- Have you trained everyone in your organization, including yourself, on the principles of finance and accounting?
- Are you elevating and promoting the importance of the science of management each and every day in yourself and your organization?

"Management is, above all, a practice where art, science, and craft meet."

–Henry Mintzberg

... think about it.

Chapter 9

The 3Ps
... *Project, Program, and Portfolio Management*

"Of all the things I've done, the most vital is coordinating the talents of those who work for us and pointing them toward a determined goal."

–Walt Disney

You may ask why I didn't include this in the chapter on being effective or efficient or even in strategic and business planning. The reason for that is because the 3Ps are so important to a business's success but often misused or executed on because they are misunderstood. So, it is with this context in mind I have decided that they needed their own chapter so that we can clear a few things up and set you on the path to success.

Project, program, and portfolio management (the 3Ps) are all ways to plan, manage and track work, and to get that work done using the repeatable processes and solid controls these methodologies have. You can think of them as work "methodologies" that use sound business practices and tools that are standard across many industries and can thus be applied, learned from, and moved transparently across industries. The main unifying theme across the 3Ps is the importance of planning, scheduling, and control that helps people create order out of chaos and thus deliver planned, predictable results.

The management of the 3Ps is very similar, it mostly varies in whether you have multiple projects and how you want to control their financials, but they all need similar skills to successfully implement them. These skills are very important to the successful execution of each of the 3Ps but are sometimes overlooked. Dave Wile, in his book *The Project Management Gene*, identifies the traits of what he calls "truly artistic" project managers. I agree with many of the traits he lists, and I also believe they apply to all the 3Ps, not just project management. Traits like *creating order out of chaos, avoiding surprises through controls and management, distinguishing project from non-project work, and walking the talk,* in general, are all traits to keep in mind and apply during execution of all the 3Ps. So, with that said, let's now dive into them, starting with project management and working up from there.

Project Management

The definition of a project is: *A temporary endeavor undertaken to create a unique project result or outcome.* Projects are temporary and close to the completion of the work they were chartered to deliver. Project management is the use of specific knowledge, skills, tools, and techniques to deliver a project. The development of software for an improved business process, the construction of a building, the relief effort after a natural disaster, and the expansion of a sales organization into a new geographic market are all examples of projects.

We define projects as unique endeavors, meaning they are all different in one way or another, but the processes of project management are not unique, and all follow a somewhat standard thought process. We call that thought process IPECC, which stands for initiate, plan, execute, control and close-out, and while there are variations that have added steps to this, I have always found that this thinking and approach is always a good place to start a project. I learned that the continuous updating of whatever artifacts and plans created throughout this process is paramount to its success.

So, why is it that project management is so important to the success of a business, you may ask? Well, that's because businesses are constantly changing, and thus, there are always large and small projects going on or to be delivered, and it is where a large portion of a business's investments are consumed. The success of these projects is very much tied to the success of the company and yourself and should be managed closely. Now, let's take a more comprehensive look into IPECC and the importance of each one of these steps.

- **Initiate:** Develop a project charter and preliminary scope of work (SOW) statement.
  - o Project description, objectives, high-level steps and milestones, resources needed, roles, and responsibilities.
  - o Communication plan with RACI model developed.
    - ▪ A RACI model or chart is a diagram that identifies the key roles and responsibilities of users against the major tasks of a project. It serves as a visual representation of who is responsible, accountable, consulted, and informed on a project.

- **Plan:** Has the details on how to complete the project within the scope, time, and budget agreed upon. Uses the project charter as a starting point. The project plan is a living document that should be worked on and adjusted daily and may be revised as needed when unforeseen incidents occur or original assumptions change. It should contain the following:

  - o **Scope definition:** A full description of the project, sometimes referred to as the requirements. The major driver of scope is the features of the work and the quality level to be achieved.
  - o **Assumptions list:** Things that are still not firm at the time the project plan is developed. They change as the project gets closer to starting, and it is ongoing.
  - o **Work breakdown structure (WBS):** Describes all deliverables that are part of the project (report, prototype, system, etc.) and then weaves them into a timeline by their dependencies on each other. Some must be completed before

others are started, like pouring cement and letting it set before you build on it.

o **Schedule:** Start and finish dates, as well as due dates for deliverables. Weaves in WBS times for proper sequencing through the use of a Gantt chart.

o **Staffing plan:** Number of people and their skills needed, dates needed, and number of hours to be devoted to the project.

o **Budget:** Outlines costs for the projects, may be broken up by deliverables, including things like personnel and equipment.

o **Procurement plan:** Resources and materials to be purchased, when they will be purchased, and process for finding and evaluating suppliers.

o **Communication management plan:** Identifies and plans communication with stakeholders.

o **Change management plan:** Describes the formal process for making changes to the project, especially important to document any requirement or product changes requested.

o **Risk and Issues management plan:** Analysis of potential risks and planned responses. Connected closely to assumptions.

• **Execute:** The daily, weekly, and monthly routines and work needed to get the project done. The fine-tuning here is in balancing the triple constraints of the scope, schedule, and budget that have been agreed upon while you are dealing with things that were unknown at the time the plan was developed. Having solid risk management plans, along with some contingency funding, helps you deal with these unplanned issues, of which there will normally be a few, at least.

• **Control:** This is about monitoring the scope, schedule, and budget, trying to see things that may affect the project outcomes before they do, keeping sponsors and stakeholders informed (RACI model), and monitoring and managing issues and risks.

- **Close-out:** Ensuring the project meets all agreed-upon requirements and can be proven. Getting sponsor sign-off. Handing the project off to the implementation or operations team. Closing the project down by ending contracts and releasing resources. Doing final project review and lessons learned.

Lastly, the final Quality Review... Not included in the IPECC acronym, but nevertheless, it is extremely important to do it thoroughly at the completion of every project. There are many definitions of "quality," but basically, it refers to whether the deliverable does what it was designed to do. Quality should weave itself through every aspect of a project.

There is a difference between the quality of the project and the quality of the deliverable. The quality of the project focuses more on the process. Was there good management? Did it stay within cost, time, and resources guidelines? Was there good communication? The quality of the deliverable refers to how well the deliverable meets its intended purpose. The best way to do this is to compare it to the original scope and requirements and how the project sponsor feels or rates the final deliverable.

Here are some of the challenges to managing projects, and a few other things I wish I had known earlier about project mgt.

In a perfect world, every project would start by having the scope and requirements fully defined and flushed out. A WBS developed from scope and requirements with all assumptions and risks identified, all work defined, and then a schedule would be developed by work-sequencing scheduling. Then a cost would be determined by this actual work and length of schedule, a budget would be allocated to pay these costs, and the project would start and end on time, with no scope, schedule, or budget changes requested. Okay, now, for those of you that have done this before, you know what I have just described rarely ever happens, or at least it has never happened to me or anyone I have ever known. The actual project usually goes something like this. You get incomplete scope or requirements with a delivery deadline predetermined and a budget already decided. You are then asked to work backward into that scenario doing superhuman things to somehow deliver an acceptable outcome. What do you think sounds more like reality? I know these two examples are truly both ends of the spectrum, and as can be expected, the truth lies somewhere in the middle, so let's talk about some of the most frequent challenges you will run into managing projects and maybe a few ways to manage them when you do.

Challenges around Scope

As mentioned previously, every project has similar constraints or challenges to manage, those being scope, schedule, and budget. In a perfect world, it should all start with your scope or what you need to accomplish. As you know, your time and costs are derived from the work outlined to complete the scope, which means if your project scope is not well-defined and correct, to begin with, then everything that follows will be incorrect. Here are a few of the **scope guidelines** I have found useful over the years to make sure I start a project off on the right foot.

- Start with what we call a *minimum viable product* or MVP and work up from there. This is where prototypes should come in, showing the sponsor of the project what is going on along the way and getting feedback as you go. Better to get something working as soon as possible, get it out there, learn from it, and improve, rather than go months and sometimes years, without something for the customer to evaluate. A great example of this would be Apple's release of their Lisa computer years ago. It was the first PC to have a graphical interface, yet not many people remember it. That's because Apple released it before it was really ready so they could get customer feedback on the interface, improve it, and then immediately follow it up with the Apple Macintosh computer, which made Apple a household name. One of the best MVP examples of all time!

- Make sure your requirements or product specs are well-defined, measurable, testable, and agreed upon by the project recipient up front. This is an important step and is sometimes not done to the depth needed. Make sure all parties agree on what the result will be! Visualization and simulation can be very important and helpful here.

- Make sure the original scope requirements and any changes to them are agreed upon and signed off by whoever is the end recipient and is paying the cost of the project. Lost control of requirements and adding and subtracting without formal agreements and sign-off are the most common reasons projects fail (think "scope creep," which is when more features or scope is added after the agreed-upon scope is completed.)

- Break your requirement deliverable down into smaller pieces that can be checked and verified along the way to make sure they will meet the final deliverable requirements.

Challenges around Schedules

The key to success in this area is to be as detailed and truthful as possible, resisting the urge to shorten it (sometimes thinking of client pressure on timelines) or lengthen it (due to being risk-averse and building in too much excess time for contingencies). Here are some **time guidelines** I have learned and found useful over the years...

- Try not to start with any time constraints or targets in mind. This will help to make sure you build the time for the work needing to be done, not to some arbitrary delivery date. If you are given a delivery date, put that to the side to go back to as a requirement after you build the real or actual time summary.

- Figure out what needs to be done, and then break it down into its components. The next step is to sequence these components in the order they need to be completed to deliver the project. A simple example would be that you need to pour the concrete foundation for a house before you start to build the frame on it so that the concrete pour would be sequenced before the framing, and the roof would come after that.

- The work components are then either broken down further into tasks or sometimes just labeled tasks. Tasks are broken down into WBS (work breakdown structures), which are nothing more than procedures to do the tasks, and the time it takes to do the procedures. Be careful when doing WBS—it is easy to get too detailed in this step, and thus takes too long to get an estimate back. Also, be careful of the trap of assigning one hour to every task. If you have hundreds of tasks, and many of them only take ten or fifteen minutes, like getting approvals or routing reports, it's easy to overestimate when doing this and thus overquote the real cost of a project. The important part of this step is that you give these tasks to the experts who know how to accomplish this work, so they can give you back an accurate estimate of what it will take to accomplish the task in time and the cost, which you will set aside for the moment.

- Now that you have your deliverables, the components, the sequencing, and the actual tasks with WBS, it's time to connect it all with something called a Gantt chart. A Gantt chart is nothing more than a bar chart that illustrates a project schedule and is useful in doing time-cost tradeoffs. It shows when a task must start, how long the task should take, and dependent relationships between tasks, along with the current schedule status as the work progresses. A timeline built on a slide is not a Gantt chart because a Gantt chart is a "living" project tool and should be the daily go-to document to see what has been done, what is being done, and what needs to be done next. When used that way, it is one of the project's main management and control tools. It was used to build the Hoover Dam and to run the NASA space program, so that should tell you how powerful it can be if used correctly.

- Projects don't go off the rails in monthly increments, so why are they reported as such? As I mentioned previously, what gets measured gets done, so if you're managing project performance and delivery daily, which is the job of the project manager, then the minute a scheduled piece of work is not completed or "slips," that should be dealt with the next day. Thus, you should never fall more than a day behind without working to adjust. This is the purpose of the morning review meeting and the weekly summary. If your project slips by a month by the time you find out about it, you have other issues you need to address, not just the slippage; keep that in mind.

Challenges around Budgets

Cost is dependent on getting the first two constraints correct, otherwise, you run the risk of not having enough money to deliver the outcome. Equally as bad, you tie up capital you didn't need for the project, which could have been used to fund other important projects. Let's look at each of these a little deeper.

One of the issues projects run into is they tend to overrun on costs from their original estimate. I am sure you have all heard the stories of large public projects that have gone awry, ones like the Big Dig in Boston, which overran its original budget estimate by $5.3B or 190%, the International Space Station, which was budgeted at $17.4B and ultimately grew to $160B, or maybe the Channel Tunnel under the English Channel which cost $21B, 80% over its original estimate. Each of these projects had lots of individual challenges, but in the end, the biggest drivers of their cost overruns were the same as the ones that affect all projects: inaccurate project scoping (many times due to using new technologies that have never been used before), erroneous estimates (hard to estimate something that has never been done before), overly optimistic forecast assumptions, and unforeseen project changes (scope creep). The good news in all of this is that in today's world, with the advent of much more refined and available data, these errors can be reduced. With the use of artificial intelligence, machine learning, structured and unstructured data, and predictive analytics, you can reduce the risk of future cost overruns lower than ever before, sometimes eliminated completely.

So, what are some of the key things I have learned over the years that you should be aware of when it comes to project costs?

- Learn from past projects. Lessons learned on a project can reduce your risks on the next one. You should have a database of all past projects and, more important, how they performed and what was learned in the project management process to do better the next time. Many project reviews just review the final costs to plan, which is a nice measure, but the real learning comes in how the whole project was run. If you came in late, how can you make sure to come in on time in the future? If you came in on time, how can you come in early the next time, maybe even shorten the schedule and save project money? I find that as the biggest opportunity. Seems like when a project does come in on estimate, everyone is so amazed they don't ask learning questions so that the performance can be repeated. We tend to overanalyze projects when they miss their budget and do not spend enough time learning from the ones that came in on time or early... something to think about.

- Do spend time learning from the outside world. Scan the outside world for similar projects and costs, and don't be afraid to contact someone in the industry who has done something like what you are thinking about.

- Get the total costs, labor, materials, and overhead... Make sure it is all activity-based modeled, not just general averages.

- A word on project contingency funds. Contingency funds are usually set aside at the beginning of each project to fund unforeseen or unplanned issues/needs that may arise. Contingency funds (usually a certain % of the total cost) vary by industry, technology, risks, project manager experience, and a multitude of other things. There is no exact science to do it right. The real thing to keep in mind is if you set up a number for contingency, then large projects are going to tie up a larger part of your budget. Now, while that may make you feel like you are managing your risk, you are increasing risk to your company overall since unavailable capital locked up in contingency means you have to forgo an unexpected expense, which can be risky and something to think about. A contingency of 20% on a $100K project is only $20K, but a 20% contingency on a $10M project is $2M, which could fund some valuable things you need if it was available. Think missed opportunity cost here.

Project artifacts that are helpful to have when project challenges arise.

Before we move on to the next P, I would like to quickly discuss what I consider to be the most important "artifacts" you or your team will use in managing a project. Each one is key not only to your project's success and learnings but also for forensics if you need to examine a project that has gone off the tracks and get it righted.

- **Project Plan:** The original project charter, business case, specifications and requirements, times, costs, team, dates, outside agreements, and contracts. All the information that was needed to approve and start the project. Make sure you talk about what is included in the project in the project charter and also what is not included.
    - ○ **Assumptions:** These are listed in the project plan and are accepted as true or as certain without proof. The best way to manage assumptions is to add their proofs as they

become available and manage them as if they are different than what you assumed would happen.

- **Project Working Documents:**
  - o **Gantt chart:** Make sure you keep the original and then have a version you adjust as the project progresses, so you can see how you did, compared to the original forecast, baseline, and re-baseline as needed.
  - o **Logs:** Risk/Issues/Change logs are the ongoing management tools that PM's use to handle project-impacting things as they arise. Make sure they have dates, names of people that escalated them, names of people assigned/responsible for solving or implementing them, et cetera.
  - o **Status Reports:** Meeting documents that show when, who, why, and what was discussed, and also what the follow-ups were and who is responsible for them. This is one area where PM's sometimes fall short, and status reports are important tools that let you recall who agreed to what as the project moves along. It helps manage and prevent "organizational amnesia," which is notorious for slowing down large complex projects and programs. Automate this as much as possible; it can be taken right from a good PM tool in today's world.

These documents combine to give you the ability to look back at your project, to learn from it, to know who to thank, to see how well the assumptions you made came out, and to set up to do the next project better. They are also key when a project has gone off-track, and you need to decide either to end it or continue. When having to make that decision, it is always good to look at the management of the project so far and see what has caused the issue. If these are done correctly, and you have someone review and analyze them who is completely independent of the working team and the outcome, you can usually see if the cause was a technical issue that could not have been anticipated or a project management issue that could have been. Good to know if you are trying to make the decision to move forward on a project or end it.

In the end, the success of project management comes from a great project manager and project team that understands not only their work but also project management in general. They know the importance of using the process correctly and have the discipline to hold themselves to that. They understand that each piece is dependent on the others, so they must be right. They know that the success of their project is dependent on accurate and timely data made visible so all can see the status and that the tradeoffs of scope, time, and cost are constantly flexing with a project and thus must be managed accordingly. Now, it's time to move on to the next P, which is program management.

Program Management

Programs are not merely big projects; they are different! The key difference is in the focus of the management effort. Project management is focused on creating a deliverable as efficiently as possible, and program management is focused on maximizing the benefits realized by the organization. Program management typically has multiple projects associated with it, as well as longer timeframes.

I describe program management as an organizational capability or function that oversees a group of individual projects linked together through a shared goal or common objective. It is the process of managing multiple projects that are mapped to business objectives that improve organizational performance. Think of it this way, project managers manage individual projects to their successful conclusion. Program managers are responsible for multiple project outcomes that roll into delivery on a business goal or objective. While the success of all the projects in the program would be welcome, a program manager will have to deal with trade-offs between the projects, often moving projects in and out (canceling and starting others) due to changing business requirements.

Program management requires that artful skill set of making order out of chaos. Many programs are multiyear in duration, with projects and budgeting decisions that need to be sequenced across the years. Think of the process of program management, including more complexity, longer timeframes, larger budgets, and an expanded skill set that starts with having all the skills of a great project manager, but then adds a broader and deeper set of skills around strategic positioning, business development, and negotiating.

Program management is usually the natural progression of your great project managers, but not always. Great project managers are excellent at delivering complex time-bound outcomes. Still, in the program management world, while that is an asset, it is more about managing trade-offs between many different constituents. Thus, communication and negotiating skills, as well as deep financial acumen, are the real keys to success.

What are a few of the things to keep in mind to be successful in program management? Think of these…

- The three qualities most needed and used in successful program management are leadership, organization, and communication.

- Similar steps to project management: following the initiate, plan, execute, and close-out steps, not as heavy on the controls since those are implemented more at the project level.

- Let the project managers manage their projects and resist the urge to micromanage them if you come from that background. Remember, if you hire great people, your job is to enable them to be successful, not do their work for them, or attempt to.

- Make sure you always have a prioritized list of all your projects, with their status. Note cross-project dependencies. When you must urgently pivot due to unforeseen business circumstances, you will find this very handy.

- Your prioritized list of projects in the program should always be agreed upon with your internal funding partners and your external customer-owning partners. Do not assume things or make decisions for people; make sure they are on board.

Finally, I cannot overstate the importance of having a great program management tool that is kept up to date by the individual project managers. Having the online capability to see the status of all the active projects, especially when they are global in nature, and allows people to always update and access information, is extremely helpful. Having one that allows you to roll all the information up and then view it in multiple ways for analysis and reporting will give you key insights into your opportunities for improvement and also save you many hours of exporting to other tools to do this analysis and reporting work.

Now, onto our final P, portfolio management.

Portfolio Management

A collection of projects, programs, and other work that is grouped together to facilitate the effective management of that work to meet strategic business objectives. The projects or programs of the portfolio may not necessarily be interdependent or directly related.

Portfolio management is very different from either project or program management. It is not a methodology that uses standard processes and procedures that are governed in certain ways. It is more of an art form that may have some similarities to project and program management, like managing multiple outcomes and tracking many things to a conclusion; that's about where the similarities end.

Portfolio management is about selection, prioritization, and control of products or services, and its goal is to balance the outcomes of a "portfolio." While this may sound a little like program management, it is very different because a portfolio does not have a collection of projects. Project and program management is about doing things right; portfolio management is about doing the right things. Portfolio managers usually manage a suite or diverse group of products or services that are grouped into a portfolio. Depending on company size and the number of portfolio managers they have, portfolios can be grouped by product relationships, product locations, service processes, et cetera. It just depends on what makes sense for the company. Where the portfolio process is the same is really in the actions that portfolio managers do every day, which is balancing all the portfolio's needs and the portfolio's performance.

Portfolio management is something that can be very different between industries, i.e., a finance portfolio manager works on different types of products than, say, an IT portfolio manager, but in the end, what their roles do are very similar. I am going to focus on portfolio management in product or services-oriented companies, not financial ones, because they have a host of other nuances that we would need many more pages and chapters to cover.

Some of the thoughts which portfolio managers must keep in mind and be prepared to manage and answer are...

- Decide where to invest the company's money.
- Decide how to measure the return on the portfolio, usually in financial terms, but can also be in strategic terms.
- Decide when to add or cut things in the portfolio (needs-wants)
- Resist the urge to micromanage ever $$$ in your portfolio if the intake mechanisms are not that accurate. Sometimes we are counting dollars while the input data accuracy is in the thousands of dollars, this is a big waste of time.

The most challenging aspect of portfolio management is very much like program management, which is to constantly be balancing the portfolio to optimize the outcome of it. Good portfolio managers pre-think through many what-if scenarios, always planning for changes in demand to their portfolio. Portfolio management differs from program management because a program manager is working to complete projects that roll up into a final defined outcome, and a portfolio manager usually has much more flexibility to determine what goes into their portfolio to deliver their final outcome. The processes are very similar, but the choices and outcomes are usually very different.

Key Challenges for all the 3Ps

While the 3Ps all face similar challenges in the areas of scope, time, and cost for successful delivery of their outcomes, it's project management that usually faces the most. When you think about it, it is understandable because the project manager is usually tasked with the complex delivery of a product or service that is unique and, many times, has never been done before. Think about it, before a project starts, the team has come up with a plan and estimates that are based partially on past experience and partially on guesswork or hypothesis. They then commit to delivering the outcome on a hypothetical timeline where they will build in measurable milestones that may be months or years away, all based on these estimates. Talk about risk!

So, when executing on all of the 3Ps, the key questions you should keep in mind, the ones you should always be "looking around the corner" for, are…

- Do I have a connected dashboard that tells me how the project, program, or portfolio is currently performing at a frequency of updating that allows me to adjust before I have major issues?
- Is there something I have learned since I have started this project/program/portfolio that I can now use to change or adjust original charter or assumptions?
- Am I releasing my contingency funds as the project risk reduces with execution along the way so I can accelerate other work?

Another concept I want you to be aware of is that everything is not a project. We need to decide what a project is (use the definition if you need help) and then operationalize what is not a project. Continuous process improvement initiatives can be a project, or they can be overburdened by them and stifle creativity and agility. Why do we projectize things when they should be operationalized since they are done every day? If you make continuous process improvements all the time, it violates the definition of a project as a unique endeavor to make them into one. Yet, we do this all the time and stifle the agility of improvement initiatives.

3P Management... The Project Management Office

Before we call an end to this chapter about the 3Ps, we need to discuss a very important thing called the *project management office* or PMO. This stands for project, program, or portfolio management office (you can pick which one you want to apply it to, sometimes it's called a PPM), and its major purpose is to help coordinate the processes used to do your 3P work so that there is consistency across your projects, programs, and portfolios. Consistency in what you measure, how you measure it, how you will report on it, who will do it, etc., are just a few of the reasons you need some type of central capability to help manage your 3Ps, especially in complex global operations.

So, why is there such churn over having PMOs in companies, well that's because of a lack of good understanding of the value they can add, and many times because of poor execution, often driven by the fact that the leaders in the company didn't want it to begin with. Also, simply put, the centralized strength becomes its major weakness due to a tendency for centralized processes and approaches to be cumbersome and overly bureaucratic. Let's look at the pros and cons of having a PMO to get a better understanding of it.

- **Pros of having a PMO:**
  - Common repeatable processes across the company.
  - Risk reduction across the P's by using best practices and standards to measure performance and outcomes.
  - Efficiency gains across project management by using standard artifacts and having standard training.
  - More efficient resource use across departments and projects along with career opportunities for PMs.
  - Coaching, mentoring, and training optimization.

- **Cons of having a PMO**
  - Too much emphasis on process and not on results.
  - Lack of direct business accountability for results.
  - Can cause extra work for the teams.
  - Introduces overhead costs and complexity.

How do you execute a good PMO?

One of the major issues of a PMO is the initial charter of its mission, accountability, and structure. Unfortunately, a PMO starting-up is often not fully supported by senior management, for multiple reasons but mainly because this is not their background, and thus many are doomed from the start. Many a PMO has been started in reflex to too many projects not being done correctly or missing their commitments, and thus the PMO comes in as the savior through rigorous project or program controls. This is exactly the wrong reason to start one. The best reasons to start one are because you are doing projects well, have seen that project and program management are professional roles that are very valuable, and it's realized that having this capability in your organization will make everyone better and lead to increased success in your outcomes. It should be an enabler to everything you are already doing, not a disabler and viewed as a cost center.

Another thing to think about is that having a centralized PMO is not always the answer to getting some of the pros of project/program/portfolio management in your company. Sometimes all it takes is a 3P community of practice (CoP), a little more formal capability, rather than everyone operating separately, where PM's can share their ideas, get some input, and bring together their best practices. So many new social platforms lend themselves to being able to do this in companies that I recommend it as the first step before deciding to move into a centralized PMO operation. I have not seen an implementation yet where using a CoP has not added immediate value to the 3P capabilities of a company.

One last note on PMOs. If you decide to implement one, please hire qualified Project/Program/Portfolio leaders to set it up and run it. Too often, I see companies choose one of their best functional or operational leaders to move into this role or best subject matter expert (SMEs), and many times, that is usually a mistake. 3P leaders are certified and qualified professionals, like lawyers, engineers, product designers, etc., and just filling the role with someone because they happened to have managed a project in the past is a big mistake. It takes years of rigorous execution of projects, using the right methodologies, tools, and techniques to get good at it. Also, some professions, like construction and software development, have even more varied ways to run their projects, so you must think about that. Just because a project manager has delivered on their project commitments in the past doesn't make them a good leader for a PMO, for this role requires a strategist and teacher first, a negotiator and marketing promoter second, and then those delivery skills, so keep that in mind.

In the end, the design and execution of a centralized PMO capability can give your 3Ps a big boost in the right direction if it is done correctly. It should be measured and evaluated each year, not by how many standards or processes it has put in or how nice its new reporting and measurement capability looks, but by the overall improvement of the project outcomes in the company. After all, that is the true reason it should have been put in. Resist the urge to measure it just by a past issue you may have had (a project cost overrun) because once that issue is solved, you are back to trying to justify its existence again, which has been the death of many a PMO.

To achieve *Better Outcomes:*

- Are you proactively managing all three of the triple-constraints of scope, schedule, and budget?
- Are you making sure you and/or your team are using all the key project management artifacts, and using them to drive positive project results?
- Managing projects is always more about managing the team than managing the work. Have you built a great team and are you unleashing their power by enabling them?
- Portfolio and Program Management are very different from each other, are you managing them that way?
- PMOs… they are all about proper execution. Look to them to enable better performance, not just save money and control things. Overcontrol stifles speed and innovation.

Remember if you fail to plan, then you plan to fail.

… think about it.

Part III

Better OUTCOMES!

... they're about applying leadership throughout your journey, start to finish!

Chapter 10

The Challenge of Leading
... *it all starts with YOU!*

"Do. Or do not. There is no try."

–Yoda, Star Wars

Now that we have worked our way through **Part I**, and the importance of knowing yourself and your possible destination for your journey. And **Part II**, where we discussed the importance of operational excellence in helping you reach your destination and where the process of management fits in, now it is time to discuss the glue that helps pull both of those together, and that glue is leadership.

Management compared to Leadership

Before we dive into leadership, I thought we would start with a quick comparison of it to management, and to do that, I want to start off with analyzing management versus leadership. Many books like to state this as one versus the other, and that is simply in my opinion wrong. In the business world, and I would argue in any endeavor where you are attempting to get something done, you need both, and that's because they are different from each other. As we mention in Chapter 8, the process of management is about planning, hiring, organizing, budgeting, controlling, and problem-solving. But as we dive into leadership, you will find it is about this and more. Leadership is about vision, inspiration, trust, and building coalitions through and with people to get things done. This distinction reinforces that you must have both management and leadership skills and capabilities to be successful. Having just one or the other will just not cut it in today's business world. Now let's look more into leadership, its characteristics, and its implementation, and that starts with the mind and thoughts of the leader.

I know the quote with which I start off this chapter seems a little harsh. But still, the reason I love it is because it looks to address one of the main issues I have seen in leaders over the years, and that is they don't believe in themselves or their direction with enough conviction, so rather than say they will "get it done" they hedge their work with the words "I'll try to get it done" which are two very different statements. One of the 3Cs we discussed back in **Part I** is commitment and how important being committed to something is to achieve success. We have an often-used phrase for that in the business world, one that you may have heard, **"burn the bridges."** What this means is that there is no path for retreat, so get it out of your mind that if you try and fail, you can just retreat… nope, sorry. Full commitment means there is no retreating, which translates into your actions as you go forward to get it done. That usually means "adjusting your sails" as you learn but still deliver the intended outcome. Let me give you an example of this "mental" commitment and how it can translate into the amazing delivery of an outcome.

One of my favorite movies is *Apollo 13*, which is the true story of the real-life aborted Apollo 13 mission in 1970. One of the most memorable lines in that movie is when the mission commander assembles the engineering team and lets them know that they have a challenge to address to bring the astronauts home alive, which is to make a circular air scrubber out of square spare parts. During his description of this challenge, he makes it clear that "failure is not an option" since failure would mean that the three astronauts would most certainly die from lack of oxygen. As history tells us, the engineering team rose to the challenge and figured it out. Nothing is more challenging or motivating than when you have to drop all the excuses and not waste time discussing why something can't be done and get to thinking of how to get it done, period!

Another great example of this type of limiting thinking is the story of Roger Bannister breaking the four-minute mile barrier back in 1954. Roger Bannister was a top runner as a student at the University of Oxford in England. In 1951 and 1953, he won the British championship in the mile run. For years, many athletes tried and failed to run a mile in less than four minutes; in fact, so many had failed that people said it was a physical impossibility. The world record had been 4 minutes and 1.3 seconds, set by Gunder Hagg of Sweden in 1945. Well, on May 6, 1954, Roger Banister succeeded in breaking through that banner nine years after Gunder Hagg with a time of three minutes and 59.4 seconds. The real highlight of this story is that while it took nine years to beat the record, after people heard it could be done, it only took forty-six days before the record fell to his rival, John Landy. So once people realized it was possible, more did it, but why not before? This is a great example of how when you believe something can be done, it can, and when you believe it can't be done, it can't, something to simply think about…

This part of the book is about the characteristics or DNA of leadership and what that means. It is about many of the words and descriptions you have probably heard over the years and how they fit together, and how to apply them for a successful outcome. Don't fool yourself—having a great skill set or the right DNA is useless if you don't know how to apply it correctly when needed. Over the years, I have seen that the world is full of extremely smart people, but I have also seen that many of them cannot articulate their knowledge, so unfortunately, the world does not benefit from it.

As you can see, I started off this chapter with a very controversial quote: "Do. Or do not. There is no try." Some people will agree with this, and some will not. My experience has been that while it is a great learning experience to try many things, it is really the success of the "doing" that eventually separates the good from the great. While many are satisfied by saying that they played the game, the truly great ones, the ones we remember in history, like Steve Jobs,

Andrew Carnegie, Bill Gates, and Dr. Jonas Salk actually got it done. While the reasons for their success have many variables, the one trait that they all possessed was the undying belief that what they were doing was important, and they were committed to getting it done. In reading their biographies, what you will also find is that they all had the characteristic we call a positive mental attitude or PMA. Over the years, it has been analyzed, studied, and tested, revealing that being a great leader is extremely reliant upon having a positive mental attitude and believing things can be done. No matter how hard a situation appears to be, it's this positiveness that inspires others and thus drives them to exceed when others have failed. And if you question the importance of this PMA, just think about how many times you have heard someone say the following quotes:

"… are you a glass half-full or half-empty person?"

"Don't be a negative Nellie."

"Are you an Eeyore or a Tigger?"

I'll bet you hear or see these quotes on a fairly regular basis. And so, you know, they are all based on looking for that positive leadership characteristic. Now, being positive, especially in the face of adversity, is just one leadership characteristic that is key to your success, but there are others that I have found over the years that are also equally as important. Here are a few examples of them from multiple books on leadership characteristics: (*Johnson & Johnson's Leadership Imperatives, Head, Heart, and Guts, The Ride of a Lifetime, The Leadership Challenge*, and the *US Marines Officer's Handbook*).

J&J Leadership Imperatives

- Visionary
- Inspirational
- Passionate

184

- Adaptive/Agile
- Decisive
- Self-aware
- Resilient

Head, Heart, and Guts

- Trust/Honesty
- Courage
- Self-aware
- Emotional intelligence
- Challenges the status quo
- Compassionate

Ride of a Lifetime

- Optimism
- Courage
- Focus
- Decisiveness
- Curiosity
- Fairness
- Thoughtfulness
- Integrity

The Leadership Challenge

- Honest
- Forward looking
- Competent
- Inspiring
- Broad-minded
- Dependable
- Determined
- Courageous

United States Marines Officer's Guidebook, where it's all about Honor, Courage, Commitment, and,

- Characteristics
  - o Can-Do attitude (enthusiastic optimist)
  - o Courageous and Decisive (commitment)
  - o Adaptable / Inventive
  - o Integrity
  - o Unselfishness
  - o Endurance
- Capabilities
  - o Know yourself (think ASA and self-aware)
  - o Know your business mission
  - o Know your people and look after them
  - o "Walk the talk" leadership by example

As you can see, these are excellent lists with many of their characteristics overlapping, proving that no matter what industry or business you are in or how many people you are leading (even if it's just you), there are some leadership characteristics like trust, optimism, and self-awareness that are universal. Keying in on that thought over the years, I have developed my own list of leadership characteristics, and to be clear, they are not very much different. I refer to this list as the **Guiding 8**, and just so you know, I preface them by saying, **"Am I,** or **Are you..."**

- Trustworthy
- Optimistic
- Inspiring
- Curious and Inventive
- Adaptive
- Decisive
- Courageous
- Resilient

As you can see from these eight leadership characteristics, there's really nothing earth-shattering here. The power of these characteristics is in understanding each one, understanding why they are valuable to possess, and knowing how and when to use each one. I call this ability "situational leadership" (which we will explore further in the next chapter). The thing to keep in mind with leadership characteristics is that their purpose is to help you establish your credibility as a leader. It's about using them all to become a person that people believe in because if they believe in you, then they will believe in your message and help you execute on it. How do you do this? It's simple. You do this by using all these characteristics to create an environment where people flourish and can be their best.

> *"You get the best out of others when you get the best out of yourself."*
>
> *–Harvey Firestone*

Now, let's take a closer look at each of these, doing a bit of a deeper dive into what they mean, what they look like, and how each one can contribute to your success as a leader.

Leadership… "Characteristics"

Trustworthy: Trust is what I refer to as the keystone of the Guiding 8. While all these characteristics have proven to be invaluable in my leadership journey over the years, it is all dependent on the level of trust you have in your team and, more importantly, their trust in you. So, what is trust, and how do you build it? Trust is defined as the firm belief in the reliability, truth, ability, or strength of someone or something. Trustworthy means worthy of confidence—able to be relied on as honest, reliable, and truthful. What builds trust? Well, besides living the examples in the definitions, like being reliable, honest, and truthful (sometimes referred to as being your true self), it's also about being fair and consistent. Why are being fair and consistent important? Because inconsistency between what you say and what you do forms the basis of what people see of you. If you say one thing yet do another, trust gets eroded. The statement, "walking the talk," should come to your mind here.

An example of trust or lack of it in today's world would be all the controversy surrounding people returning to the office after the COVID-19 pandemic. While many business leaders are voicing their opinions on whether people are more productive in or out of office, the real issue is not trusting the team members to decide where they would be the most productive. I always like to say that if you have hired the right people since that's where this all starts, then they know, or should know, how to get the job done and where is just another logistical problem to overcome. Now, there are a lot of variables here, especially if an employee is new and may need help understanding where the best work productivity is or experienced employees who can tell you exactly what works best for them, but in the end, great leaders will work with their people to set the proper outcome goals and objectives. Leave it up to their team to figure out the best way to get that done, and anything less than that level of trust is unacceptable and will be detrimental in the long run. Think about it, that discussion about if people are productive working remotely is really about whether leaders trust the people they hired to do their work wherever they can if it's possible.

Optimistic: Are you hopeful and confident about the future. Do you see the "art of the possible" or the "pain of the impossible?" Would you describe yourself as Eeyore—sad and gloomy, or Tigger—positive and upbeat? These are questions you should ask yourself, or better yet, ask your friends and business partners how they would describe you in this context. Why is this so important? Well, who would you want to follow, someone that believes the future is bright or someone that thinks it is gloom and doom? If you are in a position of leadership, then it is part of your role to make sure people can see an overall positive vision of the future, even if there is some short-term pain involved. The hardest thing for a leader to do is to maintain their and their team's focus and optimism during tough times, but that's what is needed and what separates the good leaders from the great ones!

Inspiring: This characteristic goes together with being optimistic. Someone or something that is inspiring is exciting and causes you to be interested and engaged. People that are inspiring come across as passionate and energized and can paint that positive view of the current or future state. They possess excellent communication skills. They make people want to join the team and spur others to action without asking them because they believe in the vision and mission that the leader has laid out. Being inspiring is like adding oxygen to your team's air supply, energizing them.

Curious and Inventive: Okay, I did use two words here, but it's only because these two words are so intertwined with each other that you can't have one without the other. Think about it, curiosity is what gives you new ideas or ways to do new things or do things better. Thus, by being curious, you also use the new information you have uncovered to do new things or things in a different way, which is the definition of inventive, so having one without the other just doesn't work. Why is it important to have these characteristics? Because if you want to be inspiring, you need to know what the future could look like, and to paint that picture, you need to have the knowledge of what could be better or different. And that knowledge comes from being curious and learning and then inventing something new. See, all intertwined, as I said. Also, do keep in mind that sometimes ideas and thoughts go nowhere, but even that's okay since learning also happens from the lack of results on experimentation.

Adaptive: Do you adjust your capabilities to the challenges and opportunities that present themselves to you, or do you try to solve things the same old way. My favorite colloquialism here is, "If all you have is a hammer for a tool, then everything will look like a nail," meaning that if your toolbox of experience is small, you will try to solve problems with only a few basic tools. More experience and knowledge garners better tools, expanding your skill set and filling up your toolbox with more of the right tools. The broader your capabilities in solving problems (gained through knowledge and experiences), the easier it will be to solve them since you will apply the right tools to the right situation. Although it is true you could use a hammer to drive a screw into a piece of wood, wouldn't it be easier with the right tool like a screwdriver?

Being adaptive means adjusting your skills to meet the current situation or challenge, often in an agile way, and this only comes about by constantly learning and growing as a leader. There are so many examples of adaptive or learning systems in the world today. From simple systems like your online purchasing history, which adjusts what is advertised to you, or more complex, like self-guiding aircraft that constantly recalculate to the input from a GPS signal. Still, the real power is applying this new technology to help you as a person and leader become more adaptable by learning quicker and then adjusting by changing course or accelerating. Think of it this way, when you make commitments, do you figure out how to deliver on them regardless of how the situation changes with subtle shifts in direction from what you have seen and learned? If yes, then you are adaptive because that's what adaptive people do!

Decisive: Are you achievement-oriented with a bias towards action? Do you make decisions and move forward without complete information? Do you hate waiting around for something to happen? If these statements describe you, then you are well on your way to being a decisive leader. The description of a decisive person is someone that can make decisions quickly and effectively. Being decisive is about honing your decision-making skills on both big and small decisions and is a critical step towards becoming more adaptive and driving positive change. Decisiveness in leadership is about making decisions with less than 100% of the data in front of you to do so. Making some decision, be it a good one or a not-so-good one, is better than making no decision at all. Why is that, you ask? Because if you make a decision, and it is the right one, you will have done something to move forward or solve an issue. If you make the wrong decision, then you will learn that decision did not work, and thus, next time, you will not make that same mistake, so learning from your bad decisions is equally as important as learning from your good ones. Still, no learning happens from no decision, just longer timelines and delays. Lastly, do keep this in mind: making no decision is a decision; you have decided to do nothing at that point, which many times also has ramifications.

Courageous: Years ago, I looked at the term courageous as a fourth C to go along with characteristics, capabilities, and commitment, but my years of experience eventually taught me that this was a characteristic that almost all great leaders possessed. How did I come to that conclusion? It was after observing different leaders either make a tough decision, one I knew was not easy for them, or sometimes the opposite, where the leader needed to make a tough decision, or take a risk or change and decided not to for multitudes of reasons. One way this is described today is this, do you run towards the fire to help or away from it in fear or safety... think about it.

Being courageous usually means taking personal risk along your journey. Overcoming the fear of failure and the need for safety (think Maslow's hierarchy of needs) often overrides doing what you know is right. I can't say enough about how important it is to be courageous when needed by overcoming those fears, both real and perceived. It's a leadership characteristic that is very visible, directly contributes to you "walking the talk" as a leader, and the outcomes of you being courageous are usually best for all.

The definition of courage is the ability to meet danger and difficulties with firmness and resolve. Wondering if you are courageous? Here are a few thoughts I have used over the years that help me determine if I was being courageous or not.

"Do you avoid the tough road or the tough conversations that are hard to do but lead to better destinations?"

"It's better to ask for forgiveness rather than permission because you learn little when someone says no to your creative idea."

"What would you attempt to do if you knew you would not fail?"

I know when I look at people I consider heroes, they all have somehow overcome the odds against them by taking risks, doing the hard tasks, and exceeding expectations. I mention the word risk here because anytime you take on a challenge or opportunity, even when failure could cause you and your career harm, it requires a level of risk-taking and bravery that many people avoid. That's why having the courage to take these risks is so important to being a leader. Blindly following orders from those in position of authority above you is no excuse for doing something you know is wrong. While doing what is right can sometimes be painful in the short term, and can be risky, it is never wrong to do what you know is right. An important thing to know about risk is to understand your own personal risk tolerance. Know if you are currently a risk-taker or a risk-avoider because you can learn to be more of a risk-taker if you need to be and thus learn courage over the years, it just takes some faith, oh and taking some risks!

Resilient: Someone that has this characteristic is someone that can recover quickly from difficult conditions. Think of it in tandem with courage because many times, after you have had to be courageous, you also need to be resilient to recover. Anytime you've had to use your mental, emotional, and physical reserves to overcome something, it becomes imperative that you have the resiliency to recover; otherwise, you may have nothing left for the next challenge, and this can lead to burnout. When I think of resilient people, I usually see people that are realistic, have self-control, keep calm under stress, have positive relationships, and take care of themselves (self-care). They normally possess a few other leadership characteristics like optimism and adaptability. Resilient people also have the self-confidence to accept the occasional failure because they understand that no matter how much they prepare for success, sometimes they will lose. This is part of life and competing. Resiliency has become increasingly important over the last few years during these trying COVID-driven times as people have had to adapt and completely change their routines and how they think about business. Those who have handled all this change the best have shown true resiliency.

As we finish this section on the **Guiding 8** leadership characteristics, one of the most important things I want you to keep in mind is the phrase "leadership by example." What this means is if these are the traits and behaviors that you truly believe in, then you need to live them each day because people see what you do, not just hear what you say. Remember, actions speak louder than words! That means you need to live these characteristics, not just talk about them and ask others to have them; you need to be "coachable" yourself to develop and deepen your characteristics. You also need to *have empathy for all people at all times* since everyone deals with challenging issues at some time, so anything you can do to help people is always appreciated.

Although it is important to know what the leadership characteristics are, the most significant aspect of being a great leader begins where we started this book, which is, with an accurate self-assessment of yourself and your leadership traits. How well do you know your personal strengths and weaknesses? What have you heard from others about yourself? What have past managers said? How about friends, partners, and past business associates? As always, the importance of an honest and accurate self-assessment is a great start.

Leadership... "Discovery"

Back in Chapter 1, we briefly talked about the power of doing your accurate self-assessment (ASA) to help you identify or "discover" your defining characteristics. I always like to start with that data because it is a snapshot of information about me from people I know and respect and from some formal analysis tools with lots of research and years of proving behind them. Self-evaluation tools like Myers-Briggs, Clifton Strength Assessments, 360-degree feedback surveys, etc., are all valuable tools in getting a good grounding on where you are currently in your leadership characteristic development. All these assessments give you small pieces of information about yourself that eventually lead up to the story of you, whether you like it or not (I will say right now that self-denial is the biggest flaw most human beings have, especially executives, and thus the most significant opportunity). They are also good for tracking your self-development by taking them repeatedly and seeing if the results have changed as your experience grows deeper and wider. My one recommendation here is that you make sure your assessments are recent, say within the last three years, since the world has changed so much in that time frame, which means you have to. And make sure one or more of the assessment tools that you use is behavioral science-based (psychology, neuroscience, sociology, etc.) to get a richer picture of yourself.

These types of tools focus on learning more about your leadership capabilities and styles, help you have the best overall assessment of yourself, and allow you to see how your characteristics match up to the important leadership traits. They can give you what I like to call an *accurate leadership assessment* (ALA), which, when added to your ASA, gives you a well-rounded picture of strengths and opportunities.

Now, before we move on, I do need to mention that all this analysis can have a few pitfalls you need to be aware of. As I mentioned previously, way back in Chapter 2, people tend to overreact to the results of their self-assessments, trying to explain why their results are good or bad. Also, people will try to characterize others by the results of these assessments, not understanding that these are just snapshots of data and do not define the person. Keep this in mind as you learn from your results and hear the results of others. It's all situational to each person, so trying to classify yourself and others is a lot less valuable than just trying to understand them.

Before we move on, I would be remiss if I didn't mention one more characteristic here: **bias for action.** A bias for action is a key descriptor that comes out in many leaders or leadership situations, especially situations where decisiveness is needed, yet is usually not listed as a characteristic (although sometimes you will see a high sense of urgency listed, which is close). We talked about the importance of being a decisive leader and having a bias towards action means not just making decisions when you have to. It's also about looking forward and working to anticipate what's next, whether it be the next opportunity or crisis, so you can prepare for it and be ready. It's about not sitting on your accolades and laurels, thus potentially inviting complacency in your team and others.

So, having a bias for action is very important to your success as a leader, but do keep in mind that while a bias for action is important, action without a direction or plan is just wasted energy and is more likely just a reaction, which is usually referred to in a negative light. Your focus should be on "responding" to significant and non-planned opportunities or issues as they arise and then applying intelligent action, hopefully from a pre-thought-out game plan to solve or take advantage of the opportunity.

Leadership... "Exemplified"

In today's hyper-competitive and fast-moving world, you need to bring your best "self" to work, life, and every day by being the best version of yourself possible. While it was deemed essential in the past to work as hard as you can for as long as you can in the macho business culture that rewarded this type of behavior, it has now been proven that the law of negative returns kicks in with this type of behavior. What I mean by this is the quality and output from people and teams that have worked too long of a day or week diminishes, and thus, the quality of their outcomes drops, leading to negative results for all. Therefore, certain industries, ones where the quality of the outcomes could lead to death if they roll off (think of airline pilots and long-distance truck drivers), are highly regulated when it comes to working hours by day and week.

Being a great leader means always remembering that you need to lead by example or "walk the talk" at all times. To do that, you must bring your best at all times, and being your best starts by keeping yourself in your best mental and physical shape so that when needed, especially when something stressful presents itself, you have the capability and capacity left to handle it. It is making sure you have taken the time to "sharpen the saw," as Stephen Covey calls it in *The 7 Habits of Highly Effective People*. It means taking the time to rest, learn, exercise (this can mean something as simple as walking or something as complex as a marathon, that's up to each person), eat healthy, and take time for yourself for whatever gives you joy. In this last one, your mental health comes into consideration along with your spiritual self, and they are equally important as the physical self but often overlooked.

People are all different, and thus, their approach to being their "best selves" may be different, but there is a commonality to things like getting enough sleep, eating healthy, and recharging oneself because we all know what happens when our batteries run low. We should act more like our devices sometimes; when our battery gets down to 20%, we should be aware, and when we get to 10% or below, we should make sure we recharge as soon as possible because we know what happens when our devices get to 0%, right?

Leadership... "Derailers"

As we get close to ending this chapter, I would be remiss if I didn't mention a few of the leadership "derailers" I have seen over the years, so let me go ahead and do that.

During your career, you may have picked up some habits that will not serve you well moving forward on your leadership journey.

- **Passing the buck** (avoiding taking responsibility): I think you all know what this is, and it is not good. The mark of a true leader is taking responsibility or the blame when things go bad and passing the praise to others when things go well. Not much more I can say about that.

- **Overcontrolling:** Being in complete control of everything when it was just you to control was great, but now that you lead or manage others, it's time to learn how to trust. Overcontrolling or micromanaging are not terms you want to hear describe you, so keep that in mind.

- **Conflict avoidance:** This reinforces what we discussed about being courageous. You usually know what the right thing to do is, but do you have the courage to do it in the face of adversity?

- **Power hungry:** Did you get into management for the betterment and gain for yourself or to help others? Do you look at everything to see what's in it for you or how it is useful to others? Are you looking to move up or be recognized for your own prestige, or to help others even more? The choice is yours.

- **Perfectionism:** When it was just you, this was a personal choice and may have felt good since it is also connected to being in control. When you are leading or working with others, it may not be such a good thing, so be aware of that.

Some other Key Thoughts on Leadership

- The word "ego" is not a dirty or bad word, although it is many times used with a negative connotation. You need a healthy ego to be a leader that wants to achieve and accomplish things. A person's ego is about their self-esteem and self-importance, and when these are in balance and driven by being a servant leader and helping others, that's a good thing, and when they are off balance, that's a not-so-good thing.

- With ego, there's a fine balance between confidence and arrogance. Which side of the line are you on?

- Always stay humble and helpful.

- Everyone deserves the benefit of the doubt, so always assume positive intent.

- Do not be afraid to ask for help, we all need it sometimes. Knowing when to ask for help is a true sign of a confident and experienced leader. As I like to say, "We win and fail as a team, never alone!"

- Being honest, open, and vulnerable is all a part of bringing your true self to whatever you are doing. Humans are not robots, although in the past, we have been asked to be that way at work. Understand this, live it, and allow it in others. It is what we call "authentic" leadership, be that if you can!

So now that you know what some of the key leadership characteristics are, where do you stand in your leadership journey as far as possessing the characteristics and developing others? What are some of the other key leadership thoughts you should keep in mind? The next step is to apply them, which we will discuss in the next chapter since having great knowledge and capabilities is a real waste if they are not actively used, and we know what a bad word "waste" is, don't we?

To achieve *Better Outcomes:*

- **Leadership...** **"Characteristics"...** Are you... Trustworthy, Optimistic, Inspiring, Curious, and Inventive, Adaptive, Decisive, Courageous, and Resilient?
- **Leadership... "Discovery"...** do you have a "bias for action"? Are you itching to get started, or content to watch others?
- **Leadership... "Exemplified"...** *"Be your best"* by living the best version of yourself!
- **Leadership... "Derailers"... are you aware of them and working on overcoming them?**

The world is changed by your example, not by your opinion.

... think about it.

Chapter 11

The Honor, Understanding, and Challenges of Leading Others
... *leadership applied!*

"People don't care how much you know until they know how much you care."

–Anonymous

You have been entrusted with managing and leading the resources of a company when they give you the title of Manager, Director, Head of VP, etc., or in your own company when you "hire" your first employee. The question is, do you see it that way? Do you understand the impact you can now have on the lives of others? Do you have a passion for helping others achieve their goals? Do you put others' goals and accomplishments ahead of your own, or do you align them with yours where possible? If you are answering yes to these questions, then you have already moved towards the mantel of leadership but understand having leadership characteristics or "DNA" is not enough, it's *leadership behavior* or *applied leadership* where the true essence of a leader comes out!

The Honor of Leading Others

Yes, always remember that it is an honor to lead others, and you respect that honor by continuously learning, growing, and using your leadership characteristics and capabilities. That's what applied leadership is all about.

As I mentioned earlier, management is considered "overhead" in the COGS formula and a non-value-added activity or "waste" in lean thinking. Thus, managers need to be working to constantly add value to others or the process, and that value should start with helping the resources they have hired be better at all times. How do you add value as a leader? Well, first, you have to understand more about leadership and things like motivation, self-actualization, et cetera. What formal training have you had in leadership? It's always quite amazing to me how important leadership is to the world in general, yet how little actual formal training goes on in this important area. Reflect on your education and training in high school, college, your first job, et cetera. Something's missing, right? What do you really know about leadership? What have you been taught versus what have you observed and learned through on-the-job training?

Going back to the chapter on the process of management, we described management as a science and leadership as an art, and this simple statement reminds us of why that is:

> *"People join a company, or a cause, because of great vision and purpose, people leave a company or cause because of poor and leadership."*
>
> *–Anonymous*

In his book, *On Becoming a Leader*, Warren Bennis defines leaders as people that know how to leverage their strengths and compensate for their weaknesses. They also know what they want, why they want it, and how to communicate this to others to gain their cooperation and full support to achieve their goals. They understand themselves and the world around them and leverage their wisdom that comes from knowledge and experience. Most importantly, they know they have been given the responsibility to lead people and all of the accountability attached. Now, let's look further into some of the things that leaders do and how they get things done.

Leadership… "Applied"

Leaders use their leadership characteristics to help their team accomplish a goal. Whether it is sports such as football, baseball, or cricket or building a team to solve complex business challenges or opportunities, it's always about bringing people together to get something done. The real art, as they say, is in knowing what leadership skills to apply when to get the most out of your team. This is not easy; everyone is different, they have different life experiences, different backgrounds, different education, etc., and we won't even get into their morals, ethics, motivational drivers, and beliefs. So, how do you lead a diverse group of people? Well, the best thing to do is start with building their trust.

Let's go back to the leadership characteristic of *trust.* Trust is built through fairness, consistency, follow-through, honesty, and meeting commitments. It is built by what you do and not just by what you say. You can talk about being lean in your operational processes, but you must live lean and agile in all that you do to make it work. You can talk about the importance of timeliness, but then you need to be on time yourself, even for meetings. Just talking about things is not enough. It's so easy to see when a leader is not "walking the talk," and that disconnect is a major demotivator and impediment to things getting done. "Actions speak louder than words" is not just an idiom; it is an extremely true application of leadership. You must lead by example every minute of every day; otherwise, you are not being your true self, and others will see this. As I mentioned before, at HP, they did not believe in locking anything because if they couldn't trust the people they hired like they would trust family, then the issue was not putting locks on things; it was figuring out why they hired untrustful people to begin with. Also, as I mentioned earlier, the controversy in today's workforce about doing the work in the office or remotely is all about trust and whether you trust your people to get their job done or not, regardless of where they are.

Trust is about executing on the hundreds of daily little things as much as the big things. It is about being consistent and following through, so having self-discipline, being visible, catching people doing things right, along with saying, "I don't know" when you don't, are all things that help you build trust with your team.

Along with trust, you should be building **empathy** for the team. Keep in mind that empathy is different than sympathy. *Empathy is about understanding where others are coming from without judgment.* It is about trying to understand what it is like "walking" in someone else's shoes, which is not easy since we all have different backgrounds and paths we have traveled. Sympathy is about feeling sorry for someone, which is different than trying to better understand them. So, how do you become more empathetic, especially with a new team? Well, it's mainly by learning more about them. It's about taking the time to truly get to know them and understand them but not judging them. It's about listening. What makes them tick, why do they do what they do, why do they think like they do, and what has led them to where they currently are in life? All those conversations that we avoid yet are so crucial to making us better leaders and, ultimately, better human beings in general because the more we learn and understand about others, the better we can help them reach where they want to go.

To truly be a successful leader, one of the main things you need to be good at is in taking a genuine interest in relating to and understanding others. While there has been lots of research done on this topic, and many great books written about it, one of the best examples I have ever come across was in a book called *Zapp: The Lightning of Empowerment* by Dr. William Byham. It is a book written as a fable about the trials and tribulations of workers in a fictitious company. While I did find the book a fun and quick read, what always stuck with me was the simple layout of the book into what *sapps* people from being motivated and able to do a great job and what *zapps* them and enables them to be successful. This taught me to always look for ways to *zapp* people and ways to take away what *sapps* people. I have used these guidelines in many different situations and business areas over the years, such as sales, service, manufacturing, technology, etc., and have found them universally applicable.

What de-motivates or *sapps* people...

- Lack of trust
- Meaningless, repetitive work
- No input on decisions affecting them
- Not knowing what is going on (lack of information)
- Not knowing how well they are doing
- Someone solving problems for them
- Not getting credit for their ideas
- Lack of resources, knowledge, and skills to get their job done

What motivates or *zapps* people...

- Trust
- Challenging work with a variety of assignments
- Participation in decisions
- Being kept up to date on what is going on
- Measurable outputs
- Authority and resources to get the job done
- Being listened to
- Public praise and recognition

For motivation to work, people need...

- Knowledge and skills
- Resources (tools, materials, time)
- Direction (goals, objectives, guardrails, measures of success)
- Passionate encouragement (feedback, coaching, reinforcement)

I know when you look at many of these terms and descriptions, it seems like there is so much to learn and understand, and you wonder how you'll ever be able to remember it all and become a great leader. Well, to that, I say this: if you focus on these things over time, then over time, they will become habits, and as one becomes a habit, then you can focus on the next one, and so on. True, it will take time, and you will have many learnings and adjustments to be made along the way. Being a good leader can be learned, so if you truly want to be one, then I say get started today because the sooner, the better. An excellent way to get started is to look for a mentor, or mentors, or maybe even a formal "leadership coach" to help you along your journey.

I have found over the years that having a good sounding board, especially someone that has no vested interest in my success or failure, has been invaluable. My sounding boards helped me better understand myself, which leadership characteristics to apply when, and to have reflective conversations about leadership when needed. In this next section, we are now going to look more into coaching because this is one of your key roles as a leader. By being a great coach to your people, they will grow just as you would if you were working with one, just as your first-line coach should hopefully be your own manager, who should be helping you grow.

Leadership... "Coaching"

I like to think of coaching, or should I say good coaching, as the final piece of being a great leader. You can have all the leadership characteristics there are, and you can have great trust and empathy with your team. Still, if you can't bring it all together, or better yet, bring your team together into a cohesive work unit, then your outcomes as a team will never be as great as it could have been.

Coaching is not as easy as it seems, as can be seen by the number of coaches let go by professional sports teams every year. It takes patience, perseverance, knowledge, and above all, empathy to get a team to gel. As we mentioned earlier, to be a great coach to your diverse team, you need to spend time learning as much as possible about your people and have great empathy concerning their different backgrounds, religions, countries, families, et cetera. That is why you need to commit to being a lifelong learner to be a great leader.

Being a great coach doesn't mean you have to be the greatest athlete; in fact, there are many examples of the best athletes failing miserably as coaches, such as Michael Jordan and Larry Bird in their short tenures as coaches in the NBA, but it does mean you truly care about people and want to see them be successful.

Great coaches know how to bring the best out in people by being great visionaries, getting people to understand how the future and the direction they are heading in will help them achieve their goals. They possess a good balance between intellectual intelligence (IQ) and emotional intelligence (EQ), and now how to use both. They seek first to understand others before trying to get others to understand and buy into their direction. They know how to actively listen and try to understand what someone is saying, not just listening to respond (Ever see this? Someone starts to answer before the asker finishes their question. That's a prime example of someone listening just to respond). Great leaders understand that they have two ears and one mouth and learn early to use them in that proportion. It is one of their keys to success. Remember, when you are talking, you repeat what you already know, but when you are just listening, you can actually learn.

Great coaches always, always, always assume positive intent with people and teams they have no history with. They never believe that someone purposely did not accomplish a task; they always assume there was a good reason for the task not being accomplished and then work with their people to get it done and learn why it wasn't accomplished to assist in getting it done.

Another thing great coaches have figured out is that to be good at coaching, you have to be a good teacher. The difference between a coach and a teacher is this: Teachers help people acquire the knowledge they need to do something, whereas coaches then help them do something with this knowledge. As you can see, these two are very closely connected, and thus is why to be a great coach, you need to be a great teacher. Coaches sometimes fail because they forget to teach their people the underlying reasoning behind why things are done a certain way, thus not helping them to think for themselves, so when the coach isn't around, the team flounders. Think of the old Chinese proverb,

> *"Give a person a fish and you feed them for a day. Teach a person to fish and you feed them for a lifetime."*

Are you teaching your team to fish or fishing for them? Which is the better approach? Teaching the team how to "fish" is obviously the better way to approach this, so why doesn't every coach teach their team how to "fish" for themselves? I believe it's because they feel that if they did, then they may no longer be needed, so rather than teach you how to do things and become self-sufficient and possibly eliminate their role, they coach you through certain work and in some cases, do that work for you. Think about it: I have seen many a time when "the boss" comes in and "saves the day" by doing something their team should have done, but, in the end, had to be saved by the heroic manager, and that sums that up because that manager is not a leader. In the end, if you teach your people how to make their own decisions, think through alternative solutions, ask for forgiveness, not permission, and most importantly, that bad news does not get better with age, then you will be well on your way to creating the next level of leaders in your organization. A great leader knows their ultimate job is to grow their people so that eventually, they can be replaced by someone on the team so they can move on to their next challenge.

One of the things about "applied' leadership I have learned over the years is the importance of taking the time to explain the "whys" behind what is trying to be accomplished. As leaders, we tend to like to spend lots of time on how to do something, but the bigger return is getting your people to understand why that goal exists in the first place. This is referred to as "commander's intent" in the US military. This may take more time upfront, but I guarantee it will pay off in the end because when people understand why they are doing something and they have bought into it, they are more motivated and committed to getting it done. So, start with the end in mind, tell people "why" this end is important, ask them to help you accomplish it, and then see how awesomely they will respond if they buy into it. Keep that in mind.

Leadership... "Teams"

If you have ever had the pleasure of being part of a team, one that has accomplished something together that has exceeded what the team members could have done by themselves, one that has overcome obstacles, deadlines, and assorted other challenges, then you know what a wonderful feeling that is. Nothing is more rewarding and satisfying than being part of a high-performing team where everyone is pulling their load and having fun. So, how do you, as the team leader, make this magic happen? Let's take a closer look at that here.

As I mentioned earlier, everyone is different, and thus, they need to be managed and led differently, but as part of a team, they should have one thing in common, and that is accomplishing their mission. Whether it is defined at the beginning of a year as their annual goals and objectives or as a project with a defined beginning and end that is much shorter or longer than that timeframe, accomplishing that mission is what the team is all about and where the satisfaction comes from when the team is successful. It all starts with knowing what you need to accomplish and then putting the right team players together to make it happen. Nothing is more important than making sure you get the right mix of people with the right skill sets, knowledge, and team-player characteristics to start the team off on the road to success.

In his book, *The Ideal Team Player*, Patrick Lencioni talks about the ideal team player and the three defining virtues (or characteristics) of humility (think ego under control), hungriness (think driven and decisive), and intellect (think capabilities), and the importance of staffing your teams with people that have all these virtues, or at least a team makeup that possesses them. It is a small list that I believe is very important to the outcome of the team, and it has been my experience that without these three virtues being visible and lived up to, most teams will struggle to succeed. Why is this, you ask? Let's discuss that some more.

As I mentioned, hiring the right mix of people to be on the team is one of the most important things you will ever do. But before you do that, you must make sure to spend time identifying what capabilities people will need to get the job done. And even more important, what characteristics you are looking for in the people you will be choosing to "play" for you.

Let's go back to the 3Cs we started with back in Chapter 2. Remember the importance of those to your own career success and how it was helpful to identify which ones you had and which ones you needed to grow? Well, that's applicable here. When you are putting together a team, you need to think through the characteristics you want the people to have so they can be successful. Do you want them to show a track record of being good team players? Do they need to be able to handle stress because you have tight timeframes? Do they need to be able to work with minimal supervision? Do they need to be able to work remotely for long hours? These are all things you need to think about as you assemble the team.

You will have different needs depending on the mission or deliverable at hand, so just make sure you take time to identify what you need since the characteristic mix will help the team gel. What I have seen as the biggest mistake over the years is in spending too much time getting the "technical" skill sets to get the work done, like type of engineer, type of programmer, type of bricklayer, and not enough time on the soft skills end of team player. Soft skills include qualities like being a good communicator, good record keeper, optimistic, decisive, etc., which directly contributes to the fact that over 50% of project work is late and over budget. Over the years, my experience has taught me that it is always better to hire the best athlete—the one that is flexible, agile, and both broad and deep in knowledge and experience—than the "idealized specialist" that is super deep but lacking in some areas. The reason for this is obvious when the game shifts or you have a need for someone to temporarily fill the role of someone else, the flexibility and agility of your team's individual capabilities are what will make or break your success, so keep that in mind.

As you pull together your team, or maybe even before that, it pays to understand a little history or background about "teams" in general. To understand more about how teams function in today's world, it pays to look back in time, back to when teams were called "tribes." Tribes were formed way back in the ice age, and that formation is what helped them survive that dangerous time. They did so by relying on each other and specializing in their assignments in the tribe (hunters, farmers, water gatherers, healers, etc.) because they knew that everyone couldn't be good at everything and there was only so much time in the day to perform their duties before it got dark and even more dangerous. (Talk about the ultimate time pressure!) Now, fast forward to today and look at how we function in society, see any similarities? See how things like neighborhoods, schools, sports teams, and businesses all have many of the same traits as tribes did many years ago, such as identifying themselves by department, location, function, position, et cetera? That's mainly because tribes got things done, and understanding this history and the similarities to managing a team will help you lead.

So, why is it that tribes got things done, and good teams get things done? It's because of their focus on a well-defined outcome with the understanding that failure is not an option and each team member has a role they play. Thus, there is a reliance and trust that has been established to make it all work. Exceptional team leaders understand the importance of these two things. They do whatever they can to make sure the mission or deliverable is fully understood before and during execution and that each team member is operating at peak performance. Team leaders start great team performance off by fully understanding what they are being asked to deliver and then by defining the roles needed to make sure they deliver that outcome. They then put the team together and work with them in refining the process to deliver the outcome and slowly turn everything but the final accountability of the outcome over to them. If the leader has done their job correctly, the team members are the real experts and should be able to self-govern and take it from there. Thus the role of the team leader is now to be the ultimate coach and servant leader, working with the team to get them what they need to be successful and then get out of their way.

General Stanley McChrystal, in his book *Team of Teams,* identified four qualities in special forces teams that I think should be kept in mind by all team leaders as they rely on smaller, more nimble teams to get things done, and they are:

- **Empowerment:** A bottom-up structure as opposed to a command-and-control model. Let the team run itself!
- **Shared Consciousness:** Understand the mission and how to achieve it.
- **Bonds of Trust:** As we discussed, focused on a strong purpose or mission.
- **Sense of the Whole**: Awareness of the entire playing field, understanding the big picture.

Teams are like tribes: they are building blocks of something larger. A baseball team stands alone in playing the game and achieving something, but they do it in the context of the division they are in and then the league they are in. A sales team is the same—achieving their sales goals and quotas may be the way they measure success, but again, it is in the context of being part of a larger company that has many more teams like marketing, manufacturing, R&D, et cetera. So, while the team does need to be focused on its mission to achieve its assigned outcome, you need to help them keep in mind the larger picture, the sense of whole or awareness of the entire playing field so that they can adjust and possibly help others as needed. This "broadness" of thinking will help your teams work better with other teams and, more importantly, help them prioritize scarce resources between teams by understanding their "interdependence" on each other. This, in turn, helps them make better priority decisions in that broader context and allows the team to deliver their intended outcome as a whole unit, not just as a bunch of individual groups or tribes. Think about this the next time you hear someone say, "divide and conquer," what they are inferring is that a team is weaker when it is not a team, so don't let your team become divided.

The importance of team interdependence, especially project ones, means working across areas and relying on each other. Stephen Covey did an excellent job showing how relationships progress from dependence to independence to interdependence in his book, *The 7 Habits of Highly Effective People,* published over thirty years ago. Interdependence is understood by many sports teams and tribes alike. They know the sum of all the parts working together achieves a greater output than those parts working independently. This wisdom is something we could practice more in business and society today. Too often, we see societies that have so much more than others or business areas that are successful while others in the same company are not. You see them competing for resources when they should be working together. Thus, they sub-optimize the whole for optimization of their area, which not a good thing.

The key to interdependence is to think "win/win," which has been written about many times over, but I have seen it rarely used. Good teams and teammates understand this, and they constantly try to do what is best for the team and for the individual, which is a tricky balance that great leaders excel at.

Leadership… "Challenges"

Many years ago, back when I was a director at Hewlett-Packard, I heard a quote that has stuck with me my whole career:

"Before you are a leader, success is all about growing yourself. When you become a leader, success is all about growing others."

Not exactly sure who said this, but to me it is the true essence of the honor of leadership. Whether it was leading a USMC squad through hours of tactical training, leading a team of technical service engineers in building a world-class support organization at a start-up, or building a team of IT leaders to support and grow a global supply chain capability at a Fortune 10 company, what I learned through all these years is that it was never about me. It was always about the team. True leaders understand this and live it every day, which is the essence of what is called servant leadership. What is servant leadership, and why do you hear so much about it today? Let me try to explain.

Servant leadership is a style of leadership in which the leader focuses on their followers' needs over their own. It is about understanding that you have no leadership without followership and that followership comes from helping others be successful.

Now, I'm not sure why this has made its way to being the new "buzzword" of the last few years, but my feeling is that great leaders have always known this. They understood that having leadership characteristics was a nice thing, but unless they knew how to apply them correctly when and where they were needed, it was all wasted.

Leadership has always been about serving others. Think about it, have you ever read a book on leadership that doesn't reinforce good or great leaders focus on getting your mission accomplished by taking care of your team and leading them correctly? I must say, the new focus on servant leadership is good to have, it means more people are recognizing its importance, but I just wish that everyone wasn't treating it like it was new. What we should be asking is, why are we discovering this again? How did it get lost before, and what are we going to do to make sure that doesn't happen again? We owe that to people, and it is one of our challenges.

Now understand being a leader or in a leadership position is not for everyone. While it can be extremely rewarding to see your team be successful and growing, it can also be extremely frustrating because of lots of the challenges that come with leading. These are what I believe are the top five challenges you should keep in mind as you grow in your leadership role…

- When you are the leader, **your time is no longer your own**, it belongs to the team you are leading, and thus, you need to be as available as possible to help them with whatever they need. Being completely unavailable is just not an option. Although, if you have hired the right people and led them correctly, then they should be able to make most decisions without your input. But sometimes, there are personal things they just need to get in touch with you about, and you need to be available to discuss those.

- **Taking the blame for your team** when they make mistakes, especially from those outside your team, can be dangerous for your career and something you need to think about before you take on the leadership mantel. Remember, the captain of the ship is always responsible for what goes on in the ship and pays the price when things don't go as planned.

- Having to **constantly be "on"** as a leader, realizing that everything you say and do will be watched and evaluated, can be tiring and unforgiving.

- **Getting people to work together for the good of the team** by putting themselves second to the team is not something people find intrinsically easy to do. Maslow's hierarchy of needs starts with safety, and getting people to feel safe and trustful is not easy. Also, one of the challenges that primitive tribes faced was the difficulty communicating with other tribes because they spoke different languages. That is the same with teams. Getting everyone to understand each other by speaking the same or similar language is a constant challenge for a team leader, and it can be exhausting.

- Sometimes the company or situation you are in is **working directly against you being able to apply the leadership and life skills you know are right**. When this happens, and you have exhausted all avenues to rectify this difference or obstacle, you have to decide to either compromise yourself (morals and ethics) or move on. Which one would you do?

Situational Leadership

As we close out this extremely important chapter, I'd like to discuss a term that you may have heard about, and if not, you at least should be thinking about as you travel along your leadership journey, that being something called *situational leadership.*

Think of situational leadership as when a leader adapts their style of leading to suit the current work environment and/or the needs of a team. Sometimes you have a brand-new team, and you need to be more of a teacher than a coach and be very hands-on. Sometimes you have a very experienced team, and you may need to be more of a guiding coach. Along with this, the environment you're operating in also influences how you lead. If things are running well, then maybe your team needs less of your involvement, so you become more of the guiding force. If things are not running as well, maybe you need to be more hands-on and be that player-manager that you sometimes see. If the outside environment has a big change, like a downturn in the economy, maybe your team will need to see you more so you can calm their fears. Lots going on around situational leadership, so remember to keep aware of all the internal and external influences on your team and adjust your style accordingly while remaining true to your core values. Trying to be the heroic leader that is always leading from the front is long and gone, but knowing when you may need to be in the front or helping from the inside or rear is an art form that you should work on perfecting. And that is situational leadership.

"If your actions inspire others to dream more, learn more, do more and become more, then you are a leader."

–John Quincy Adams

To achieve *Better Outcomes:*

- Do you truly **feel it is an honor** to lead others?
- **Leadership…"Applied"**: Are you applying your characteristics and leadership principles to help others be successful?
- **Leadership…"Coaching"**: Are you applying the correct coaching of the team, or are you doing their work for them or being too directional?
- **Leadership…"Teams"**: Are you harnessing the power of teams by leveraging their diversity and inclusion to get the best results?
- **Leadership…"Challenges"**: Are you rising to them or hiding from them?

"The pessimist complains about the wind. The optimist expects it to change. The leader adjusts the sails."

–John Maxwell

… *think about it.*

Chapter 12

Leading Change, Communications, and Time
... beware the leadership quicksands

"You can't reach what's in front of you until you let go of what's behind you."

–Anonymous

"Change is hard" is an interesting statement I have heard from many people over the years, whether it be small business owners, large corporation executives, or even individuals involved in something other than business. And I do agree that some changes are very hard, especially ones forced upon us because of medical or family reasons. Now, to the leaders that say change is hard while leading their normal day-to-day business responsibilities, I say this, "Change itself is not that hard or difficult; it's our approach to that change that makes it hard, starting with our mindset."

Think about it: how many times have you heard coworkers or your manager or someone at the gym start with that statement: "Change is hard," just before they start telling you about some necessary change? How does that make you feel? I'll bet it raises your anxiety about what is about to come next in the conversation, doesn't it? Rarely do people leading change break it down and give you the details around what part of the change implementation is hard, right? The real issues around what is wrong with "change" usually center around people not agreeing with the change, not understanding it, not liking how the change is being implemented, not being involved in its planning, et cetera, and thus, they resist it because of all these reasons. That's what we will talk about here. Change is not that hard but leading and implementing it is, and thus, it needs to be better understood by all, especially those that are tasked with leading it.

To begin with, we need to fully accept that change is everywhere and that it is no longer an event—it is a part of life, and thus, getting good at changing is something everyone should accept and strive for. Whether you are an entrepreneur, new manager, seasoned executive, or part of a team, accepting change must happen, and embracing change is paramount to a change's success. I mentioned above some of the reasons that changes are not successful to start with, like people not understanding the change or not having been involved in its planning. There are many other reasons why changes are not successful, such as the changes not being the right ones or not being done for the right reasons. But the main reason change initiatives fail from the start is because the person or people responsible for making sure the change happens are not good at explaining the *whys* behind the change. This is a critical step in getting individuals or teams committed to any change, and without that commitment, changes fail.

Want successful change? It starts with explaining the *whys*

Think about successful change initiatives, ones where you have driven them, been part of a team that has, or even one that was personal to you. Have you ever thought about why they were successful? I'll bet it has a lot to do with your buy-in or the team's buy-in to that change, where you have committed to it. Where does that buy-in or commitment start? It starts with understanding *why* that change must be done to begin with. The *why* of a change has many beginnings. It could be a normal planned event driven by something like your annual business plan or New Year's resolutions, or it could be from an unplanned event, like a client's business shift or a shock to the system, like a health issue that requires you to change immediately. It could be from something simple, like wanting to paint a room in your house because you are tired of a color, or it could be something complex, like wanting to move to another country for some reason. No matter what the cause of the change, understanding that *why* behind it is the first step in gaining commitment to it, and it's that commitment that will start the process for a successful change.

So why is it that we are not good at explaining the *whys* around a change? Well, there are many reasons. A very simple one is that, as children, we used to ask "Why?" a lot. But the answer to that question was so often, "Because I said so," and after a while, we just stopped asking. We perceived that those in authority (like our parents back then and our managers now) knew more than us, and we didn't have to know. It is what I call a *learned response*. Another one is around the mindset I mentioned, with leaders not realizing or accepting that change is a universal part of whatever they are doing. Thus, change management is their responsibility.

Because of that flawed thinking, they never get good at leading change because, many times, they outsource it to others both inside and outside the company. One more reason is that even if you are good at leading change, many change initiatives will directly affect people in both a positive and negative manner, and human beings are programmed to avoid conflicts since it invokes the fight-or-flight response in us. So, explaining changes that need to be implemented, especially ones that will affect people in a negative way, are avoided or outsourced, so the person who is responsible for that change does not have to look like a bad person or feel uncomfortable. This is where the leadership characteristic of being courageous is needed most but, unfortunately, is not executed as much as it should be.

The Process of Change

Like I mentioned earlier, we tend to make change harder than it has to be because of our thought process or just our plain inability to explain the *whys* behind the change. No matter the reasons for our inability, becoming good at changing and leading change starts with adjusting our own mindset or thinking differently, and that will lead us to talk about it and eventually leading change differently.

So, how do we change our own mental mindset? Well, that's by keeping a few thoughts in mind that should pop up as soon as you hear about a change initiative or realize you will need to lead one.

- Do I fully understand why the change is needed? Will it lead to a better future?
- Can I explain the above reason to others and lay out the envisioned future so that people buy into it?
- Changing with the times and leading those changes is part of my job; it is never outsourced or delegated. I owe that to my team and myself.

These are just a few of the simple thoughts I always quickly referred to whenever change was upon me. How you personally feel about a change that you have been asked to lead or be a part of will also directly affect your ability to lead it. Changes that can affect people's lives, like organizational reductions, are the hardest to implement. Many times, these types of changes are disguised or communicated as change initiatives, which is why so many people have negative connotations attached to past change initiatives, so keep that in mind. Being truthful with people is how you have built trust with them and yourself. Not being truthful to them or yourself will erode this trust over time and lead you to an unsuccessful conclusion on many of your change initiatives if you are not careful. Be brave enough to admit you don't have all the answers or details worked out and secure enough in your leadership to ask the team for help in doing this as you move forward.

"Change is scary but staying the same is even scarier!"

So how will you know if you have made the "shift" and accepted that change is not that hard and ready to get good at leading it? Well, like I said, that will be when you start to hear your words changing, along with the telltale sign of where you are spending your time and energy. What I mean by this is, do you spend your time constantly justifying the change, playing defense to it, and not sure if it is the right thing to do? Have you embraced it, can explain its positive impact to others, and are leading the implementation around it? If it's the latter, then you have moved on to the positive change leader plateau, and that's what leadership is all about.

Now, I know some of you are thinking I am oversimplifying this because change can be a lot more complicated in some cases, and to that, I bring up the point from this perspective. I do agree that, in some cases, change can be very hard on people, but I also say that those are the corner cases, and the majority of changes we need to implement are just made harder because we think they are. If every change initiative just stopped leading with the statement "change is hard," more changes would be successful faster because people would start from a positive perspective of the change. The sooner you shift to this thinking and help others to also shift, the sooner you can move into the process of change, and that starts by building commitment to it, whether that be for yourself or for others.

Speaking more about the actual process of change, I always like to start out by pointing people to one of the most influential books I have ever read on change, John Kotter's *Leading Change*. In this book, Kotter covers many topics around change management, diving deeply into the psychology of change and how to accept it and do it well. He defines an eight-stage process for creating major change that starts with establishing a sense of urgency and ends with how to anchor the change management process in your culture. It's important to create both a sense of urgency and an envisioned future for the team to gain their commitment, which are two steps Professor Kotter mentions in his eight-step process.

Building Commitment to Change

Since each person that is affected by the change is needed to make it happen, it becomes critical that each person is individually committed to the change as much as possible. As I mentioned earlier, to create this commitment, it is imperative that you create a sense of urgency with the team or with yourself if it is an individual change initiative because one of the derailers of successful change initiative execution is taking too long to implement the change. Thus, the change "dies on the vine," as they say.

So, how do you prevent taking too long? That's by making sure you understand the improved vision of the future the change will bring. Always keep that envisioned future in front of you so that when the change initiative gets tough, people get through it by seeing what the outcome of that tough time will be. Thus, this helps them stay the course!

Commitment to change travels through very distinct steps as it progresses, those being...

1. **Awareness:** Individuals become aware of the change and a vision of the future that is introduced.

2. **Understanding:** Individuals can explain the impact of the change on themselves and on the organization and why things need to be changed.

3. **Acceptance:** Individuals have a positive attitude regarding the change and can see themselves in the new state. They begin to feel accountable for making it happen.

4. **Adoption and Ownership:** Individuals champion the change, taking accountability and ownership for the success of the transformation, and now look to improve upon it.

...and a plot of that looks something like this...

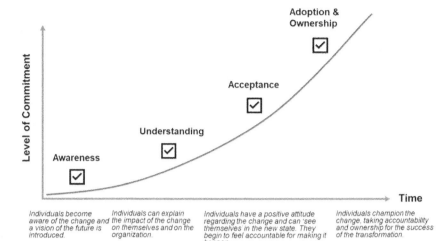

Trying to skip or circumvent any one of these steps or implementing them outside the order they are in will make the change you are trying to implement that much harder to get done, so it is highly recommended that you methodically work your way through each one.

So, in doing that, what signs should you look for that show a certain step is moving in the right direction? It goes something like this:

- When people are beginning to be **aware of the change,** you will start to *hear them talk about the change.*

- When people **understand the change,** *they will start to think differently,* and you will see this in their language and questions.

- When they move into **accepting the change,** *they will start to behave differently,* doing things like using new data sets, looking for different measures of success, and making new recommendations around the change.

- When people have **adopted the change** and are driving it, *you will start to see different results and outcomes.*

- And finally, when people have taken **ownership of the change** and have it fully functional, they will feel proud of it, accept it as their own, and look to improve it.

When you put it all together, it looks something like this, and do notice that once a change moves to acceptance, it really starts to accelerate the level of commitment of the team, or this could be the inverse—is the team's acceptance causing the adoption acceleration? Something to think about.

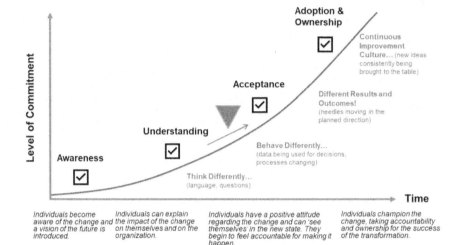

What more can I do to shift thinking and move people up this curve quicker? I would focus on the following things:

- **Communication:** Set expectations, explain the *whys*, and align accountabilities. Get the information you need to communicate about the initiative and the resulting value it brings. Provide team members with clear expectations on the outcome they need to deliver.

- **Training:** Provide the skills needed to implement the change, explain in detail, or at least lay out the potential *hows*. Listen to what training the team requests after the change initiative starts. Many training requests are unplanned for at the beginning of a change because of unseen needs, so be flexible to add in more training where needed.

- **Engagement:** Check for understanding as you progress. Involve colleagues and stakeholders throughout the process. Invite feedback from those outside the team as you progress. Keep the outcome or goal in front of the team and yourself.

- **Follow-up:** Provide feedback and future modification suggestions. Celebrate small successes along the journey as well as at the end. Ask for input on the next change initiative process.

- **Awareness:** Be aware that even though you have changed and realize that change is not hard if you accept and embrace it, others, many times, do not see it that way. They will need help and assistance along the change journey to constantly remind them of the positive final result the change will bring and why it has to be done. Also, be aware that change will always have its "detractors." People who just do not want to change for many reasons, and thus, you will need your intestinal fortitude to overcome that resistance to keep the change moving forward.

Communications Management

As you can see, one of the most important pieces of a good change program or initiative is having a great communication process. Yet as I mentioned, this is one of the areas that change programs seem to struggle with, so why is that? Well, my experience has led me to believe it's because of the lack of emphasis we put on successful communication as part of every leader's job in general, just like the lack of emphasis on change management as part of the role.

Think about it, when was the last time you saw people moving into management be required to take a communication or writing class? Is it a determining factor in promotion? Should it be? Communication is such an important part of being a leader, yet for many of the leaders I have spoken with and many of the managers looking to move further up the leadership ranks, it seems to be something that is not focused on as much as it should be, until that is, it becomes a problem, or it is mentioned on their annual performance appraisal. I don't know how many executives and managers I have talked to over the years that were perplexed when they were told they needed to improve their communication skills, but that's all they were told, and thus, they were not exactly sure what to go work on.

So, what exactly are communication skills, and why are they so important? Think about this:

"The single biggest problem in communication is the illusion that it has happened."

–George Bernard Shaw

I heard this quote early in my career, and it has always stuck with me, mainly because of the simplicity of its message and the true ease of fixing it. Communication is defined as the imparting or exchanging of information or news between persons. The challenge is in this exchange, which, if not understood, can give us the illusion that communication has taken place. Why is that? Think about it. If you are speaking to someone in English, and they only speak a language other than English, then even though you say something to that person, you have not really communicated.

While this is a simple example, think of that in the context of work when someone comes in from a different department, say engineering, and they are talking to the finance team. How much of what the engineers are saying do the finance people really understand? How likely are they to admit they don't understand? If you take this into the home, for those of you that have teenage children, think about how many times you speak to each other yet, due to many reasons, don't understand each other. See how easy it is to have that illusion that communication has taken place.

Now let's make this a little more complicated with the different types and ways to communicate, which are verbal communication, written communication, visual communication, and nonverbal communication (where you observe a person and infer meaning, see how complicated this can get?), all with their own challenges.

Verbal communication, as many will attest, is the most difficult type of communication because, most of the time, it is a mix of verbal, visual, and nonverbal, especially in today's video-driven world. While there are many ways to become good or better at it, starting with formal training and courses from universities and vendors. The best way to grow in this area is simply by practice and repetition. There is no better substitute for "stage fright" in presentations than to continually find situations where you can do it, with good practice and rehearsal beforehand. Fear of presenting in front of an audience is always highly ranked as one of people's top fears, and it's only through continual practice and doing in this area that you become more comfortable and better at it.

Like I just mentioned, communication takes many forms. Still, the most important thing to remember about communication is that not only do you need to be able to speak and present your topic or point in a compelling and understandable way, but you also need to go on the opposite side of that communication path and become a good listener.

One of the great fallacies of being a great leader is that you also need to be a great orator. While this is an important characteristic, and you do need to master it as a component of your leadership capability, equally as important, and some will say even more so, is your ability to be a good listener. Listening is a skill where you should be using a combination of your senses to "hear" what someone else is saying. In a presentation, what is the content of what someone is saying? Does it make sense? How are they presenting it? Is there energy and conviction to make you believe in it? What are their nonverbal signals saying? Do they believe in what they are saying? Does it show? Listening skills are an integral part of your leadership capabilities, and in combination with your speaking skills and your observation skills, along with your empathy, make up your whole suite of communication skills.

While we are seeking to become better listeners, better speakers, and improve our empathy, it is also good to keep in mind that, like change management skills, the first step to improving your communication skills is for you to understand they are an integral part of your leadership capabilities and that means you own them! Many leaders, over the years, have, for some reason, decided to outsource this important capability to others, thus having communication teams or departments centered around doing this. While that may make sense for external communications, especially for public companies that must be aware of what they say and do because of government rules and regulations, I'm not sure it makes good sense for internal communications.

Why I say that is this: if communication is a key part of being a leader, then the leader should always be working to improve all parts of it, verbal, written, and visual (presentation skills). For some reason, usually, in the name of efficiency, you see the last part of that given to others to do. Now, while that may be okay at the most senior level, where you have to do maximum time trade-offs, the issue is when that happens at the more junior level. Thus, the early-stage leaders and new managers never really develop their capability in the written communication area since they have someone else doing their messages for them. Keep that in mind as you look to develop yourself and others—words and writing count! I see lots of opportunities here, especially in today's world of spell checkers, grammar correctors, and so on in the digital world. And things like texting don't help us, either. Although it does speed things up, bad communication can do more harm than good, so be aware of that.

Now, getting back to some ways to be a better communicator. Here are some other ideas I always keep in mind:

- Listen, learn, lead (what I call L3): one of the sincerest forms of respect is listening to what another has to say to learn and understand rather than to just reply. Be willing to change your point of view if needed.

- For communicating important changes or any new initiative, it's always best to explain the *whys* with the resulting value they bring, connect today's performance and the changed outcome, set expectations with times, and then align accountabilities with team members.

- Excellent communication skills will make you a better coach by allowing you to send your messages so they will be better understood and received.

The last thing I want to leave you with in this section is to never underestimate how many times you need to repeat new messaging for it to stick. People have a lot of things going on in both their work and home lives (business and personal), and thus, it takes consistent repetition of new things and lots of patience to get change to stick, and communication is key. Multiple ways of reinforcing something new should be implemented using all the communication ways available to you, such as talking about it (town halls are great for this with lots of time for questions), sending messages about it, doing videos about it, and so on. It's the only way to break through all the other messaging vying for people's attention every day.

Numerous studies have been done on communicating new messages, and they all have come back to say that you need to repeat your message at least seven times to people for that message to stick. That means they must hear it that many times, which is the more difficult part to get to happen. You must think of it as social marketing and the many ways to do that if you want the message to be heard and to stick!

Time Management

Ah, time. Such a simple concept to understand but one of the hardest to use correctly, which is why there are so many time management courses. So, let's talk about why time is so important and maybe some ideas on how to manage it better because let's face it, we can't create more of it (twenty-four hours in a day no matter what), and we can't get it back once it has passed (not yet at least, time travel, anyone?). Thus, managing it better is the only lever we get to pull. As I love to say, "The bad news is that time flies; the good news is that you are the pilot!" which means that although you can't change the speed of the plane, you can adjust its course along the way to make the ride that much more enjoyable! Another point I want to bring up is why time management is essential, and that is not only because time is bound and limited, but more importantly, the lack of controlling one's time, or losing control of it, is one of the biggest stressors people have in their lives, and one of the biggest reasons they leave or change jobs, so being good at it has loads of rewards.

So, what is the first step in managing time correctly? Well, that's in trying to control as much of it as possible. What do I mean by this? Well, many times, your time is not your own, unfortunately, due to the role you are in at home or at your place of business. Now, you could say you own your time, and no one can make you do anything with your time that you do not want to, and technically that is true. Still, as you know, there are some commitments that we have made previously, like having a family, being a doctor on call, or being part of the senior team of a public company, which means that you need to be available at a moment's notice for something you may not have planned for, and thus you lose control of your "schedule" or time when that happens. So, what can you do about that?

First thing you need to do is to understand that you may be in a role where your time is not your own and either be okay with it or not. If you are okay with it or accept it, then you can move on to what I will discuss in a moment, which is how to manage your time around that.

If you haven't accepted that, then let's talk quickly about it. Over the years, I have seen many successful people, and the ones that are the most successful always have an uncanny ability to have their time under control. In talking to many of them over the years, some very recently, the overriding factor to their success, they point out, is that they say they made peace with the time constraints that their chosen path has on their lives, which includes every time they have changed roles or careers, and thus, they worked everything else around that. In thinking of the power of that statement, it led me back to our earlier chapters around the 3Cs, deciding early on what we are good at, where we want to be, and what sacrifices we are willing to make to travel down that path to the planned future. To me, this seems to be the key to starting your time management growth. Do you accept where you are with the control of your time or schedule, and do you want to work to maximize the operation of that, or do you not accept that and thus need to change your path or current circumstances? Not an easy question with no easy answers here, but one I recommend you explore if you seem to never be able to get any control over your time. Now, let's move on to how you can potentially manage the time that is your own.

How to Better Manage your time

Managing your time starts with a very basic understanding that any time you waste cannot be retrieved, period. With this understanding, the next step is to then understand that managing time is about making choices and getting good at making choices, both easy and tough ones. That is what great time managers do. So, how do you get better at making choices? Well, that starts with making and always having a prioritized list of what you must get done, starting with what you value the most and then working down that list and reprioritizing that list as you go. It's a process that, when followed, can really help you get and stay focused on the things that are most important and valuable to you, and it looks something like this...

- **Make a prioritized list** of what's important to you.

Start by answering the question, *"What do I value the most and am not willing to compromise on?"* Is it your health, your family, or some hobby that you love? Is it your business or career? Whatever it is that makes you the happiest or gives you the most satisfaction should be at the top of the list. This does not have to be just one thing, the top few things on your list may be all about you, your family, or even your friends, but the important thing is to make sure they are prioritized. The biggest issue I have seen here over the years is people's inability to prioritize the things that are important to them, having them all as equally important. Unfortunately, this failure to prioritize leads to the inability to make sound choices when needed at critical times. Better to take the time to prioritize now than to be forced to have to do it too quickly later with less thought and planning.

- **Fill in your calendar** from this prioritized list.

Before you can fill in your calendar, you have to decide how many hours a day, week, month, or year you want to spend on the things you have defined that are most valuable to you. To stay healthy, have you blocked out seven to eight hours a day to sleep and an hour of the day at the gym or to walk, meditate, et cetera? To start a business, did you put down working sixty to eighty hours a week? Have you blocked out the amount of time it takes to get a family going in the morning and then to end the day with them? These are the types of things you need to timebound and then fill in on your calendar, so you can see what time you have left to work with. Also, don't forget to block your time for vacations, holidays, family visits, travel you know about and want to do, events with friends that you know about, etc., so you have a true idea of what time you have left to get to the next level of important things on your prioritized list.

Hopefully, you have enough hours to do everything you need and want to do. If not, then this is where ruthless reprioritization needs to begin. Better to manage this upfront as soon as you know there will be conflicts than to let it be until the conflicts turn into emergencies of which you now may have limited choices.

- **Ruthlessly manage your time to your priorities.**

Not someone else's. This is where the greatest conflicts arise. Negotiating and creativity skills become extremely valuable here.

Does your job require you to be at the office or some other place certain times or hours of the day? Are there important meetings that happen at a certain date and time of the day every week, month, or year? As you have all experienced before, many times, your job or career time requirements are in direct conflict with your personal time requirements. Unfortunately, too many times, I have seen that the personal time requirement is the one that gets sacrificed first. This is where choice comes in, and yes, you have one. What I say is this, do whatever you can to keep the higher prioritized item as often as possible, and be willing to discuss this with whoever is looking to interrupt it.

Let's say that you are scheduled to be in a meeting every morning at 8 am, yet you would like to drop your child off at school at least a few times a week, or maybe you are a single parent and absolutely must, then the thing to do **is not** immediately make this meeting schedule issue your problem. What I recommend on time conflicts is that you learn how to approach whoever is impacting your current prioritized schedule and ask them to move it, with a good explanation of why or even compromise and see if you can make it only a few times a week. Too often, we immediately sacrifice our own priorities, ones needed to help us be a better version of ourselves, without having this conversation. You'll be amazed how many times you'll be able to work out a very acceptable compromise to these conflicts once you start to protect your time more.

- **Repeat this process.**

Repeat this process on a daily or weekly basis, depending on how dynamic your personal or business environment is, until either all your open times are filled in (trying to leave weekends open as much as possible or blocked for only what is important to you) or all your "have to do" items are done.

Don't forget to build in "think" time to be creative; it's like a mandatory meeting with yourself and is so important to your creative and strategic thinking capability. Too often, this gets moved to the "want-to-do list" rather than the "have-to-do list," and I vote against that if you're doing it.

After all your "have to do's" are done, then you can expand out your "want to do's," although those are the ones that rarely any time is left for, sorry to say.

A few last things to think about. One is that the toughest part of this process is not filling in your calendar or even making your initial list. It is in continuously adding, subtracting, and moving things around on the list and in making sure the items on the list are important to you and have to be done. Most people have "to-do" lists that are very long. When I look at them, the first question I ask is, "What absolutely has to be done?" Prioritizing themselves first and then dropping things that are not absolutely critical. The next thing I ask is, "What can be delegated to others?" When really pressed, you'll be amazed how much can be delegated. Then lastly, once the list is firm, it becomes your job, like I said, to ruthlessly protect your time, not allowing others to change or impact it without your direct approval, something to think about.

Along with that thought, here's another. If you know your best time of the day, the one when your body and mind feel the best, try to put your hardest work in that time slot. That could be where you handle the biggest monetary decisions, schedule the toughest meetings, have the hardest personal conversations, et cetera. You'll be amazed

236

at how much more productive you will be and how your work and decisions seem to be less challenging. These times vary for everyone. I personally happen to be a morning person and have always done my best work from 6 am to noon, but to others, this would be the middle of the night for them, and they would much prefer to work their best from 3 to 9 pm. It doesn't really matter when this time is, just that you recognize it, plan around it, and make it work for your time management.

Let's discuss Meetings... the good, the bad, and the ugly!

Meetings, ah—talk about a love-hate relationship with a major component of all that we do in the business world. There are so many things to dislike about meetings; we have too many, they take too long, we don't seem to accomplish much in them, they give us "death by PowerPoint," they don't stay focused, et cetera. Yet, in a recent 2021 survey of over six hundred professionals, it was noted that the average employee spends almost eighteen hours each week in meetings, which means they spend over one-third of their working time on video (Zoom, Teams, etc.) calls or around a conference table. While this is not evaluated as meetings being either good or bad, the real issue when you look deeper into what people think about meetings and what the study reveals is not that they don't like the meetings; they don't like how poorly the meetings are run. So, let's look further at that.

To start with, you need to keep in mind that meetings can have multiple purposes, and it's good to make sure you understand upfront what type of meeting it is you are having or attending. The purposes of meetings are to communicate or share information, brainstorm-ideate, solve problems or resolve disputes, improve performance (a sort of problem-solving), and build teamwork. Some other definitions you may hear about are usually variations of these, ones like planning and kick-off meetings, which contain pieces of the types above.

So, before we move into how you as a leader can get good at something that you and your employees are spending a minimum of a third of their time in every week, let's look at what I call the good, the bad, and the ugly of meetings.

- **Meetings… the Good**
  - The purpose of the meeting is understood, it is deemed necessary, and an agreed upon outcome is defined, as is the outcome owner. I good question to ask yourself or the meeting organizer is, "What will we have at the end of the meeting that we didn't have at the start?" and then go from there.
  - Meeting invite has an agenda, and any pre-reads were appropriately sent with enough time to read them, not the night or an hour before.
  - Meeting is as short as possible but as long as needed to avoid follow-up meetings if possible.
  - Only the people that are critical to solving the problem or issue are invited if it is a problem-solving meeting.
  - Meeting has a facilitator responsible for not letting one or two people dominate or hijack the meeting and for keeping the meeting focused, on topic, and moving along.
  - Meeting starts and ends on time, and occasionally early because attendees are well prepared.

- **Meetings… the Bad**
  - Meeting invite arrives without purpose being defined or without an attached agenda.
  - Meetings scheduled for first thing Monday morning or end-of-day Friday, on a regular basis.
  - Meeting invites more than two layers of management, showing lack of trust and way too many people's time is wasted.

- o Meeting leader consistently shows up late, thus showing lack of respect for the meeting attendees on a consistent basis (but always has a good excuse for lateness)
- o Meeting has no one as dedicated scribe to capture meeting commitments or handle meeting drift.
- o An "unnecessary" informational passing meeting that could have been handled by a good email or memo. Many informational passing meetings are only held because people cannot depend on others to read their email; thus, they hold a meeting to make sure their message is received. This is such a time waster. If someone doesn't read their informational message, then that is their issue, and they should be held accountable or liable for that.
- o Most people multitask in meetings because they don't need to be there, and it has been proven that multitasking takes away from the problem at hand, which is why texting and driving is illegal.
- o Meeting has no follow-up message within twenty-four hours after the meeting for everyone to see what was agreed upon and who is accountable for what commitments and when they are due.

- **Meetings… the downright Ugly!**
  - o Meeting invites with no meeting purpose.
  - o Meetings are called last minute on a regular basis, and thus, other meetings must be rescheduled on a regular basis.
  - o Meeting starts late because of late arrivals and ends late because of late attendee arrivals and topic drift.
  - o Meeting issue is never solved or even understood, and the outcome of the meeting is another meeting because of the inefficiencies, so nothing moves forward.

So, now that you have some idea about the good, bad, and ugly of meetings, how do you become good at leading meetings? Here are a few thoughts. A great meeting is one with a purpose that is communicated, has an agenda, has a defined outcome, has the right attendees (in skills and quantity) that know why they are there and how they can contribute, and has enough time to solve the problem. This last part is extremely important; let me explain why. If you have a problem that you and your team have decided will take forty hours of work as a team to fix, you can solve it two ways in time. One is having a forty-hour block of together time to get it done in one week, and the other is scheduling that together time as one hour a week for forty weeks, delivering the final solve forty weeks (nine months) from the start. Which one would you choose? So, don't be that leader who schedules an hour every week with your team, and then when an issue arises, you decide to solve it at your normally scheduled weekly meeting for however long it takes. Be the one who truly lives in the agile world, decides with the team how long the solve will take, and then immediately gets together to solve the problem, thus gaining the results of the solving much earlier than the normal meeting way.

I will end this chapter with a diagram that I have used over the years, one that shows how complexity creeps in as you add more people to any equation, especially meetings and emails.

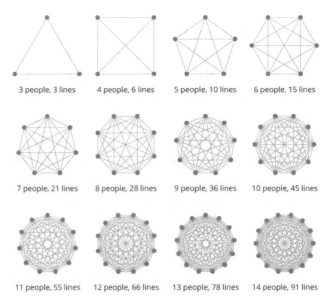

| 3 people, 3 lines | 4 people, 6 lines | 5 people, 10 lines | 6 people, 15 lines |

| 7 people, 21 lines | 8 people, 28 lines | 9 people, 36 lines | 10 people, 45 lines |

| 11 people, 55 lines | 12 people, 66 lines | 13 people, 78 lines | 14 people, 91 lines |

As you can see from the communications diagram, the more people invited to a meeting, the more complex the lines of communication get, and thus, the greater chance of misunderstands happening. Keeping your invites to the bare minimum needed to solve the problem at hand is one of the most important things you can do for the successful outcome of a meeting.

As you have probably noticed, I have spent a good amount of time on change, communication, and time management here in the leadership part of the book. I struggled with making these three important areas into their own chapter. Many business or career books just gloss over them or weave them into other sections, which I could have done since they could have fit into the process of management chapter well, but in the end, I decided to make them their own chapter. Why? Because I believe these three things, coupled with your leadership characteristics and your ability to apply leadership, are all intertwined. If you have all the leadership characteristics and have achieved your own personal mastery, and then are applying them correctly with your team, and also have the change, communication, and time management to make it all work seamlessly, you will have achieved a level of performance that I, and others, have rarely seen through the years. Having this level of leadership proficiency, along with the honor of leading others, means that you will be able to give them a level of leadership that they deserve, one in which they will all cherish and prosper from forever!

<u>To achieve *Better Outcomes:*</u>

- In most cases change is not hard, if you change the way you think about it; are you thinking differently?
- Are you getting commitment to the change before you try to implement it by thoroughly explaining the *whys*?
- **Communication Management...** is every leader's job. Are you applying L3 (listen, learn, lead) on an ongoing basis?
- Are you listening to learn, or just to answer?
- **Time Management...** once wasted, time can never be retrieved, are you protecting your time with that thought?
- **Meetings,** how are you doing with the Good, the Bad, and the Ugly?

"It is not the strongest of the species that survives, nor the most intelligent that survives. It is the one that is most adaptable to change."

–Charles Darwin

... think about it.

Part IV

Better OUTCOMES!

… bringing it all together!

Chapter 13

Continuous Growth
... *through Continuous Learning*

"Learning never exhausts the mind."

–*Leonardo DaVinci*

As we have progressed through this book, I have occasionally mentioned the importance of growth through expanded knowledge and learning, whether it be about yourself, the processes of business operations, or leadership. Remember what I said about luck happening when opportunity meets knowledge, experience, and preparation? Well, an important part of that knowledge and preparation happens through continuous learning. So now, let's dive into that some more because continuous learning is what many people talk about, but few understand and commit themselves to.

Why continuously learn?

Continuously learning something new or something more (Which I define as an extension of something we already know. Think deeper knowledge around a topic.) is important to us because all living things grow through continuous care and feeding. Whether it be plants that need sunlight, water, and minerals or humans that need water, food, and the rest of Maslow's hierarchy of needs to survive, when things are not nurtured, fed, and taken care of, they tend to stop growing, and that especially applies to our minds.

The basis of continuous learning or any learning journey should come from the thought that the mind needs consistent care and feeding, and thus, learning never stops. Think about it. From the day you are born, you are always discovering something. Whether it was seeing or hearing something you have never seen or heard before (which is everything as a child), touching something and learning what is hot and what is cold, or experiencing something, like traveling in a car, plane, or boat, your life has been filled with many new learnings on a continuous basis. You look at the world in wonder and amazement and learn new things every day.

So, why don't we keep that wonder and amazement around learning? Why isn't learning something that just happens to us every day for our entire lives? Well, that has its roots in the fact that as we grow and experience things, they become more standard and routine, and thus, our mind begins to just accept what is there and loses that inquisitiveness that comes from sensing things for the first time. We lose that early sense of discovery and wonderment, having seen the same things over and over again; thus, we become less awed by them and less able to discern the new and amazing from the repetitive and standard (and boring).

Why is this an issue? Well, that's because if you stop learning, especially in our day-to-day endeavors, you mentally stop growing and become stagnant, otherwise referred to as "we've become comfortable." Why is this not a good thing? I like to think of our minds as an infinite storage container, ready to be filled with new thoughts and observations each second it is awake, and the only way to do that is to constantly use it. Now, if its use is confined to what it already knows and has done many times before, it becomes disinterested in new things, which we refer to as stagnation. Why does that happen? Mainly because new learning causes the brain to have to work harder, and like it or not, our brains are just like the rest of us as we age; that hard work starts to be avoided because it is uncomfortable for us. Thus, over time, we lose the excitement of new learning, wanting to just "stay where we are" in the name of comfort.

A good example of this is how your body reacts when you change your daily routine of using your muscles. If you are a walker for your exercise, or a biker, climber, hiker, et cetera, think about what happens when you change your routine. Something as simple as changing your walking route from a flat route to one with steep hills causes you to work a little harder, right? Then the next day, aren't your muscles a little sore? Well, that's because you changed your routine, and the muscles you hadn't been using now got used, and they are letting you know they didn't like it by creating a little lactic acid in your (okay, overly simplistic here, but you get the point). Now, if you keep that new routine, you will build up those lower-use muscles, and the pain will eventually go away. Thus, you will have gained something new, but it took a new experience and some uncomfortableness to do it. That's how you should think about learning and your mind. The more you do things differently, the more you try new ways of doing things, and the more you will develop new ways of thinking. These new ways of thinking will then lead to you expanding your capabilities and, over time, hopefully, lead you to new and better outcomes, or at least different ones.

Think about how you do things every day, especially at work or in your career in general. Have you been doing the same things the same way for a long time, or do you look at each day as an opportunity to do things in a different way? Do you have twenty years of experience and learning if you have been in your role, company, business, or career for that long, or do you have one year of learning twenty times? It's knowledge and learning that enables the former and prevents the latter. Have you been stretching your capabilities and adding to them daily, weekly, monthly, and annually by learning and doing things differently? If yes, then you are a continuous learner.

So, why doesn't learning happen for everyone on an ongoing or continuous basis? The reasons are many and varied. Some of the recurring themes are:

- **We are learning for the wrong reasons...** lots of time just to check a box, get a certificate or other piece of paper, or because it was forced upon us at a certain job.

- **Learning the wrong things...** topics that are not applicable to what you need, say management training for someone not interested in being a manager.

- **Learning at the wrong time...** we tend to schedule learning in a haphazard way, fitting it in around other more important things, thus devaluing learning.

Thus, we learn and forget (we will dive more into this later in the chapter on the process of learning). The last recurring theme that I have personally heard over the years, the one that bothers me the most, is, "We are (or I am) too busy to make time for a course, a book, a video, et cetera..." to which my answer has always been, "It's your funeral, see you there."

Remember, your thought process should be that learning never stops. You now know the "why that shouldn't happen," so let's see how you can make learning happen!

How do you make "continuous learning" happen?

The first step in making continuous learning "happen" really starts with the mental shift that moves the importance of learning to the top of your thought process. Too often, we say learning is important, and we reinforce that by going to college, getting certificates, hiring people with degrees, etc., but then when we plan our strategies or allocate our financial resources, we put education and learning at the end of the list. Sound familiar? How often have you experienced training being at the top of the list for what needs to be done to be successful? How often have you seen your training budget preserved and protected, and funded first at your company? Pretty rare, huh? Unfortunately, it is usually the opposite. Think about it. You come out of a strategic planning offsite, and people are focused on the goals they need to achieve and how they are going to do it by changing the way they do things, but do they start by saying, "The first thing we need to do is upskill and retrain our current employees that got us where we are today, so they can help us get to where we need to be in the future." If so, then you are one of the lucky ones because, unfortunately, this is much lower down on the implementation list of many companies or businesses and usually turns into "What is the minimum amount we can spend in this area, so the other areas have the financial resources to be successful?" I always look at this as being counterintuitive. If your number one expense in a company is your people, then it has always occurred to me that anything you can do for them that will make them smarter and more productive in their roles is the best spend of money there is. Makes sense, right? So, this is your number one opportunity; change the conversation from just talking about the importance of continuous learning to implementing it each and every day in everything you do. Here are some of the ways to do that.

It begins by understanding that there are many ways to learn. The best thing to do is to first figure out what the team needs to learn to do their job better or differently if it has shifted, then work with them to provide the medium they learn from the best. Ways to continuously learn:

- **Make time for it.** Go back to the section on time management in this book, where we discussed prioritizing the things that are must-do's and add it to that list. If feeding your mind by learning is not on or near the top of your list, then you need to ask yourself why? If the reason is because you are, or think you are, the smartest person in your company or room already, then time to find another company or room to be in.
- **Make it timely.** Just-in-time training is the best. Learning decays with time. I'll expand upon this more in the next section.
- **Try different learning methods.** I like to group learning into a few simple areas or methods to keep it simple, and I recommend

you try them all and find the ones that fit your style and learning process the best.

- o Formal learning
  - University and college courses (degree or certificates)
  - Professional licenses (law, engineering, etc.)
  - Industry certifications (Six-sigma, lean, project management, certain technologies, etc.)
  - Technical certifications (CCNP, C++, Python, and other programming languages)

A note: If you are going to take the time to train in something, go the extra step and get an industry-recognized certification. If you need it for a next job and you don't have it, it's too late. And no one wants to hear, "Well, I took the training, so I know the info. I just don't have the certification." Certs will never hurt your career. Although, do make sure your learning is measured by the outcome of the new knowledge, not just by having a new certificate.

- o Informal learning
  - Industry conferences
  - Local professional chapter meetings
  - Ted X meetings
  - Master class and other online presentations
- o Constant learning
  - Daily reading, personal and professional
  - Nothing beats getting better at observing what is going on around you in your environment and reflecting on why things are what they are. Start simple. Can you name the bird that just flew by or identify that smell you just experienced? It's hard to do that if you are constantly looking down at your mobile device.
- **Try different learning formats.** There are many ways to learn: in-person at a school or event, remotely online (YouTube, Zoom, Master Class, or Teams, anyone?), podcasts, on-the-job training (hands-on with an experienced person or automated

guide), reading, video, combinations, et cetera. The more ways you use to learn, the more fun it will be, and the more the new learning will stick.

The Process of Learning (PoL)

Yes, like many of the things we have talked about in this book, learning has some distinct process steps that I like to call the "learning loop." (Although, I will say that continuous learning in the "constant" sense is best done unstructured, so no process necessary there.) The loop goes like this.

- Decide what you need or want to learn when
- Learn (see previous section)
- Use the new learnings
- Get feedback on the results of the use and evaluate
- Refine the learning
- Repeat the process until desired outcome is achieved

Pretty simple, isn't it? Although, the challenge is in having the discipline to execute a few simple steps *inside* each of these steps to make sure you get them right. Let me explain.

- **Decide what you need or want to learn when**

There are two components in deciding what you need to learn when. The first component is *what*. What is your learning reason? Is it to expand your knowledge to solve a current problem? To prepare yourself for the future? To expand your mind as a person? Identifying why you need to learn something is an important step because that will help you identify to what learning depth you need to go. To do this, I recommend you investigate single-loop and double-loop learning, a process identified by Harvard professor Chris Argyris in the nineties. The power of this thinking is that if you ask yourself why something is happening enough, you will get to the root cause, not just settle for solving a symptom of it. Thus, this is what you would look at to learn more about and change. Too often, we stop asking why when we get to a reason that is comfortable to us, and thus, we don't get to the real root cause, so we solve the wrong problem by learning about the wrong things. Yes, this can get convoluted here, so I do recommend looking into this further.

Another way to discover what you need to learn is through applying the Pareto rule, which says you should focus your learning on the 20% of things that you need to do 80% of the time. It's not saying the other 80% of the things are not important, but the more you can focus, the quicker you can become better at something, and then you can move on to the next learnings needed.

The second component of that first step is about *when* or the timeliness of your learning. I mentioned this earlier because to make learning stick after it has occurred, you need to use the new knowledge within a certain window of time—otherwise, it will fade away. To explain this phenomenon more, I refer to the chart here by German psychologist Hermann Ebbinghaus, who pioneered studies of memory in the nineteenth century. This chart is a representation of his discovery of the "forgetting curve" and that wonderful expression we refer to today as "use it or lose it." Yes, that does have its basis in research like this.

The Forgetting Curve

If new information isn't applied, we'll
forget about 75% of it after just six days.

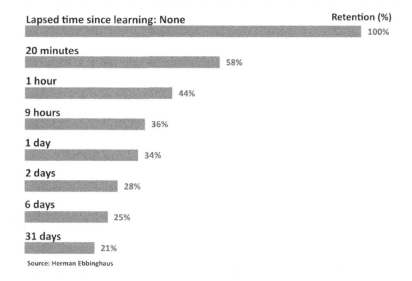

Lapsed time since learning: None
Retention (%)
100%

20 minutes
58%

1 hour
44%

9 hours
36%

1 day
34%

2 days
28%

6 days
25%

31 days
21%

Source: Herman Ebbinghaus

So, as you can see from this chart, the sooner you use your new learning, the more of it you will be able to apply, and the better the results of its application should be. This is why hands-on programs that reinforce what you learn by doing are so successful. It's the basis of why some learnings, especially the trades like electricians, HVAC, plumbers, etc., all have very in-depth apprenticeship programs because some knowledge has no replacement for hands-on learning.

- **Learn**

Continuing the implementation of the learning process after deciding what and when you need to learn. That is the step we have become very good at over the years, and you can refer to the ways of learning I identified previously if you want a few reminders there.

- **Use the new learnings**

Now we move on to the most important part of the learning process, which is using the new learnings. I can't say enough how important this step is. Learning something new and then applying it in a timely manner that uses the new knowledge in a productive and measurable way is what learning something new is all about. Did you look further into types of birds so you can identify them the next time one flies by, and did you? Did you learn a new way to coach people, and are you trying to use that new way to be a better coach? Can people see your improvement, or do the surveys say you have gotten better at it? Applying your learning as soon as you can and figuring out how to measure its impact are two very important pieces of the process.

- **Get feedback on the results of the use and evaluate**

I have seen more training programs be dissolved, not because the training wasn't needed or wasn't good but because no one could figure out the results of the training. Lean learning is about learning the right thing at the right time and for the right reasons, and outcome measurement is the only way to know if you got those right. Also, measurements of training success are something I highly recommend you decide on before you take the training because learning something new without determining how you'll know if learning has happened really is a waste of money and will eventually cause your training programs to lose their effects and also be dissolved.

- **Refine the learning and repeat process until desired outcome is achieved**

Ok, you identified what and when to learn something, you have learned it, have now applied it, gotten feedback on the results, and measured it, and now it's time to either declare success by moving on to the next new learning you need (remember this is continuous) or to adjust your training if the outcome wasn't what you expected. The choice is yours in this step. Many programs do measure the results of what they trained on, some by just counting how many people were trained, the best by measuring the outcome of the training itself, but then not many take the next step of going back and adjusting the training for the next time around. My recommendation is that you focus on doing this since that feedback can help the next round be better than the last one, and thus, the outcome could and should be better. This will set up a continuously improving training program and outcome, one that could become your competitive advantage if done correctly.

To end this chapter, I want to make this statement: *"What you do with your new knowledge is as important as what you learn."*

As I have said a few times, using what you learn in a timely manner and measuring the success of the learning is important. Learn to "apply" your new knowledge or capability, not just learn it. Is your learning allowing you to be more competitive if you are in the competitive world? Is that new learning making you a better person? Is it allowing you to have a greater impact on others and society as a whole? Is it making you feel better? Whatever the reason you chose to learn, I hope that you can see the impact of your learning and can see the importance of it. This is how it becomes part of your DNA, and you move into continuous learning mode. You see the results, they reinforce what you like or want to do, you see the impact you are having, and you then decide to do it on a continuous basis because it starts to reinforce what you are passionate about. One of my favorite sayings is, "a mind, once expanded, never shrinks back to its original form." Think about this. Even if you can't measure your training results, just having taken the step to learn more will have expanded your mind. And while it may not be in some way that you can consciously see, sometimes the subconscious remembers things that are amazing and applies them subconsciously, so no learning is ever wasted. I'll leave you with this thought:

"Never stop learning because life never stops teaching!"

-Anonymous

<u>To achieve *Better Outcomes:*</u>

- **Are you feeding you mind** today and every day by continuously learning?
- Do you have many years of learnings or one year of learnings many times?
- Are you **making time for learning** but also making sure that learning is timely?
- **Use the process of learning** (PoL): Decide what and when to learn, learn it, get feedback, refine the learning, repeat the process.
- Are you doing something with your new knowledge?

"The only way to win is to learn faster than anyone else."

–Eric Reis, The Lean Startup

... think about it.

Chapter 14

The Importance of Balance and Resiliency

"Balance is a feeling derived from being whole and complete; it's a sense of harmony. It is essential to maintaining quality in life and work."

–Joshua Osenga

Balance

Balance in every endeavor we take on in both our personal and professional life is paramount to success. Have you ever overtrained for something to the point of injuring yourself and thus could not compete in your original quest? Well, you can do the same thing when you don't balance your personal characteristics or other leadership traits.

Too much of anything is never good. Think of all the problems we have in the world because of inequalities and how things like nature would be better off if we brought our ecosystems back into balance. Think about the problems we have in the world today due to inequalities in income distribution, food distribution, and water distribution. Imagine, in the US, if we could take the excess water on the east coast and transfer it to the drought-stricken states in the west, wouldn't that balancing of water be great? We should apply this thought process to everything we do.

Balance is what we should always strive for, if possible. And I say, "if possible," because sometimes, to get that balance, the hurdles are too great to overcome in the short term, like transferring that water in the US, but that doesn't mean you shouldn't strive for it. Balance is something we should strive for when possible and aspire to when not as possible.

Why strive for balance? What happens when we don't have it? Well, that out-of-balance situation causes a myriad of problems, as the example of training some muscles too hard points out. Being out of balance is going to cause one area to exceed or excel while causing another area to fail or underperform.

Balance in our personal and professional lives doesn't mean that there aren't times when you occasionally need more of one trait than another, thus temporarily being "out of balance," but what it does mean is if you swing too far in one direction for too long, there are ramifications for that. The definition of balance is an even distribution or equilibrium of weight, amount, et cetera. Any force on an object in balance is equaled by forces in the opposing direction. A very important part is that last piece of the definition, meaning that if you move too far one way, equally strong forces will be applied to move you back to balance, and that may cause other issues.

Think about it: too much exercising of one muscle group can cause issues in others because they begin to weaken. Too much coaching of one person can cause the others to feel left out, and their performance could decline. Too much inventory of one product, or in one place, can cause shortages in others. In the end, it is figuring out how to balance all of this, how to apply just enough force to move things along but keep them as close to balance as possible, that is the real challenge.

So, how do we know if we are out of balance? How do we come back into balance and stay there? Well, I have found that the best way to explain this is by referring to the ancient Chinese symbol for balance, the yin and yang.

If you look at the symbol, you see that it has a black (yin) and white (yang) component. This duality represents the idea that two opposite characteristics can exist in harmony and complement each other.

What is often missed is the understanding of the border between these two parts, the actual line that separates them, and that's a shame because this is such an integral part of the whole meaning. Look at it closely, notice that it is not a straight line, notice its gentle "S" shape or curve, how when you move along the line, let's say from top to bottom, it goes from having a larger black portion to a larger white portion. What this represents is that they are connected and constantly flowing into and out of each other, that there can be no positive without some negative and vice versa. In total, what this symbol is telling us is that sometimes you may be out of balance, that you may need or have a little more "lightness" or "darkness" depending on where you currently are or what your situation is, but in the end, there is only one whole, and harmony is achieved when that whole is in balance.

Think about it in the everyday characteristics of people, some managers are too hands-on, or too talkative, or too nice (we often like those), and some are not hands-on enough, too quiet (not enough coaching or feedback), or too tough. This "out of balance" causes ripples in their work environment, both good and bad, and these ripples will eventually hit an object that reflects them back, hoping to put everything back in balance. The key thought here is to understand that in the long term, things will always try to get back in balance or equilibrium; thus, most imbalances are only temporary.

"Too much of a good thing is never a good thing" is another one of those statements I heard a long time ago that has always stuck with me. The reason for this is that it has been a way to check to see if I am in balance. Let me explain. When things are going well for them, people tend to enjoy the "good times" and not think about the why or how of their situation. The issue with that is the longer these good times last, the ones that are out of the norm or way above the averages, eventually, following the understanding of the yin and yang, things will work to get back in balance. What this means is the current light will travel towards darkness, positives will have some opposing negatives, and soft will travel towards hard, as the current situation travels back towards balance and eventual harmony. Heady stuff, I know, but thinking this way will make you enjoy the good times more and prepare you to be on the lookout for the offsetting times that will appear to bring back the balance.

How do you achieve balance?

By being aware of *where* you currently are on the "S" curve. "How close or far am I from equilibrium or balance?" and "How did I get there?" are two of the most important questions you should constantly be asking yourself to stay in or get back to balance. Am I way above my historical store sales? Are my customer service ratings the highest they have ever been? Are your investments at historic highs? These are the types of questions you should be asking and then looking for the *hows* behind them to see if you should be concerned. They give you the information on if you are in or out of balance.

"A rising tide raises all boats" should be remembered when performance exceeds the normal. Are you doing something that is different than what you've done before, or is the whole market up, and you are riding that rise? Do your customers really love you, or is their rating of you high because all customer sentiment is up? (The opposite of this is true, too, are your ratings low because of you or the industry you are in, like the airline industry.) Asking these questions and knowing the answers is what helps keep you in balance. In your personal life, are you making more money than ever before? Are you extremely happy because of the life that money is currently letting you lead? Why are you making so much money? Is it because the industry you are in is overpaying for people right now? What happens when that cycle reverses, and there are layoffs? Will you have saved enough money to weather that storm? The thing to work on is balancing each of the outlying performances, not by being negative or a naysayer, just by asking questions, thinking longer term, and being as prepared as you can be. As I always like to say, the negatives are never as bad as you think they are, and the positives are never as good as you think they are. Balance is where it's at!

Knowing if you are currently in or out of balance is what starts you on the journey to regain or achieve balance. The best way to get back in balance and stay as close as possible to equilibrium to achieve harmony is to make sure you keep balance in the forefront of your mind always. How do you do that? It's simple: you just ask yourself the question, "Am I in balance?" It really is that simple. If your answer is no, or if you just feel that you are out of balance, then to get back into balance, you need to analyze what is out of balance and why and apply the counter forces to them. This is the hard part. It's usually easy to identify if you are in or out of balance. Even identifying *why* you are is not too difficult. The real difficulty in staying in balance is accurately identifying what the opposing force is that will get you back in balance and then having the knowledge, ability, fortitude, discipline, etc., to do it. This is where many people need help because human nature finds it hard to stop something that feels good, or to interrupt it in any way, so don't be afraid to ask for help from others on this step.

Keep this in mind as you work on keeping in balance. Getting yourself into balance should be your first step because if you are out of balance as a person, then this leads to being out of balance in your performance, and it goes on from there.

One last thought to leave you with before we move on to the next section, *situational leadership* is about balance. Think about it. Great leaders constantly evaluate what is going on around them and how it affects their people. They are always scanning the horizon and seeing if their current leadership style is correct for the situation they are currently in and the future situation that may be coming. They are constantly looking to balance the current needs of their people with the needs they will have as the future arrives.

An example of this would be a leader that balances the team working normal hours today, say 8 am to 5 pm, with a future where they see a lot of work coming at the team. That leader may decide to give some people more time off in the near future because they may have to work longer hours in the not-so-distant future, so they are working to give some balance to the team or people by moving to one end of the "S" curve for a short time before the opposing force gets here and moves them to the other. This way, when it is averaged out over time, there is some semblance of balance for that team or person.

Resiliency

As I briefly mentioned in Chapter 1, the power of resiliency is having the ability to bounce back when dealing with unplanned events or long times of stress. It is about your capacity to recover from something difficult or challenging, to "spring back into shape," as they say. Resilient people successfully adapt to difficult or challenging experiences by using mental, emotional, behavioral, and physical flexibility and adjustment. They learn how to just "let things go" because they have prepared to do just that.

So, why is being resilient important, you ask? Well, that's because when we are stressed and anxious, we are more likely to make errors in all that we do. Recent studies show the pandemic-introduced stresses, like unclear responsibilities, conflicting information, high workloads, and time pressures (yes, very much like we mentioned before around the things that demotivate people), have caused error rates to rise as much as 500% in some work environments. These increased error rates along with the physical and psychological toll stress takes on the human body, are why having resiliency is so important.

So, how do we become more resilient and grow our ability to bounce back from stressful situations? Well, that's by understanding more about stress, why it's both good and bad to have stress, and how to "train" yourself to handle more of it.

To begin with, we must rid ourselves of the negative thought that stress is bad. Stress is not bad—it is something that appears in our normal, everyday life.

"Difficulties are just things to overcome."

–Ernest Shackleton

Stressful activities that we encounter and manage every day, like driving, managing a household, and having children, or a partner, are all things that inject a normal amount of stress into our daily lives. Where stress is "bad" is when it becomes excessive. We have trained ourselves to handle this normal level of daily stress, and when our stresses exceed the norm (increased work hours, going through a divorce, sick children, pets, etc.) for a certain amount of time, they exceed our capacity to handle them. Thus, this excess stress starts to have a negative effect on us overall.

So, how do we handle this negative stress and increase our ability to handle it? By increasing our resiliency by training for it before it arrives. A great example of this is the simulated battle exercises our armed forces run. Starting in boot camp, one of the ways our military prepares new recruits is by increasing their physical capabilities with well-designed strenuous exercise routines. These routines are considered strenuous (notice the stress derivation of the word here) because they are designed to add on to each other as the training goes and constantly push the recruits' muscles past their current limit. By adding this stress to their muscles in a controlled way, their muscles begin to build and expand, and thus they have trained them to work harder and handle more load. Not as well known outside of the people that have been part of recruit training is that while building physical capabilities, they are also expanding mental capabilities to handle stress. They do that by running simulated battle situations that introduce recruits to lower levels of sleep than normal, introducing the "chaos" of battle with unstructured situations and lots of noise (okay, and lots of yelling), and by constantly asking you to make decisions under these very stressful situations. At the end of this training, recruits are much better prepared to handle higher-stress situations, which is why the training is built this way. This situational training continues through a person's whole career in the military.

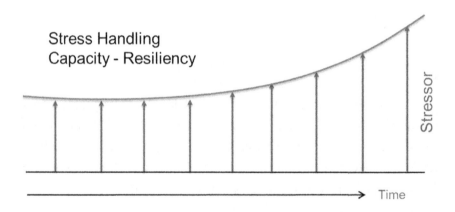

Now, let's talk more about how you can increase your own resiliency without joining the military (unless, of course, that is your chosen career path). One of the first things to do to increase your own resiliency is to understand that training to handle stressful situations is about simulating the stresses before they happen. It is about controlling and influencing what you can (like routines and schedules) and learning to let go and not worry about what you can't (interruptions, others' actions, emotions, et cetera). As an example, if you are looking to increase your physical ability, you could do that by:

- Adding more weights to your training
- Adding hills to your climb
- Adding more speed to your run
- Riding farther on your bike...

As you can see, these are things that you can control and will eventually increase your physical capabilities over time. I mention time here because if you have ever tried to increase your physical capabilities, you know that it takes time and patience, along with muscle soreness and fatigue (what I call a level of "uncomfortableness"), to build to a new level of capability. But do not try to force it too soon—that's when injuries can happen. Now, while you can control the things listed here, some of the things you can't control would be the gym times, the weather, or an injury, so just understand that and be mentally prepared for those issues if they arise.

Now, while these descriptions are fine for building new physical capabilities, what about building our ability to handle more of the mental stressors that we encounter each day. How do we expand our capability to handle those and grow our resiliency? That starts with your "mindset," looking at and handling the stresses around you differently, which goes back to what I started with, my statement that "stress is not a bad thing." If your body tenses at the first sign of stress, and your thoughts go negative, then your fight-or-flight reflex has kicked in, and "reaction" to that stress will become the norm. What if you saw that stress coming and you "responded" rather than "reacted" to it. What if you had already prepared your mind for it because you had thought lots of scenarios through and welcomed it as an opportunity to show how you can handle an increased level of stress better than before. What if you already know your default stress triggers and response and work on controlling them? Understand, I am not talking about those unforeseen and unwanted stresses like a divorce, family health issues, or loss of job, but daily stressors like increased work hours, financial challenges, unscheduled meetings, short-term loss of schedule control, et cetera. How do you train or prepare for these? How do you handle these "uncomfortable" situations?

- Proactively take on new or challenging assignments. This will help you handle change better and reduce the stress that comes from change.

- Volunteer for stretch assignments at work or in your community that forces you to occasionally work outside your normal work hours.

- Waiting for things, especially if you tend to be impatient (yep, that's me!), can be stressful. Learn to control your impetuousness first by being aware of it and then with relaxation techniques like mindfulness (living in the present), controlled breathing, and whatever else works for you. Lack of control is a stressor; learn to let it go.

- Learn something new. Lack of knowledge about situations or issues is a big stressor. Learning can reduce stress. Reading, podcasts, and videos can all be used to reduce your stress levels by making you more prepared for the future, but be careful what you watch; that can also increase stress levels.

- Think about what causes you mental stress and approach that head-on where possible. Anxiety is sometimes caused by thinking about what could happen rather than making something happen.

- Try not to worry about things out of your control. All worrying does is rob your happiness from your present state.

- Try to keep physically fit. It's been proven that your physical shape impacts your mental shape, so stay healthy.

Old way of thinking: "stress is bad and should be avoided at all costs." New way of thinking: "stress is okay," it is a normal part of life. It stretches the body and mind and causes them to expand. Constant stress is not good and should be avoided if possible because, like a machine, if you overwork your body and your mind or overstress them, they will wear out and break down.

While all these things will help you handle stress better, the other big thing to remember is to make time for mental recovery. Just like your muscles, your brain needs downtime to recover. Constant stimulation that comes at us daily overstimulates the brain, and thus planned recovery time should be part of your resiliency routine. Practicing mindfulness by taking a break in whatever way works for you is very helpful in recovery. This recovery of your mind will then have you prepared for the next stressful event that arises. Without planned mental recovery time, you will eventually become exhausted, and that's where a lot of people spend way too much of their time without even knowing it. Don't let that be you. Take that break and, better yet, combine a gentle walk with your thought break for a double gain!

A final word about mindfulness. Your body needs good fuel (food) to be at its peak form or preparation, and so does your mind. What you allow into your mind daily will affect its inner workings. Be aware of what you are reading, scrolling, and especially watching on television or in videos. Think of this as food for your mind and be aware that it will affect your thinking whether you intend for it to or not. Train yourself to see and be the "positive."

Lastly, practicing gratefulness is one of the best ways to calm your mind. There is always something to be grateful for, with the first thing every day being that you woke up. I know that sounds simple, but there are many people around the world that did not. How you get out of bed every morning and approach your day is what sets you down your daily path. It is your choice, no matter how tough or easy the day will be, so what choice are you going to make? We all have our aches and pains, our issues and challenges, our good days and bad days, but when we practice gratefulness, we also realize that no matter how big the challenges we start the day with are, someone, somewhere, always has bigger ones. Something to ponder.

To achieve *Better Outcomes:*

- **Balance...** Where are you along the "S" curve, are you near equilibrium? What direction are you moving in and why? Are you working to achieve harmony?
- **Normal amounts of stress** are good for us, its excessive stress that is bad. Are you training to grow your normal?
- **Resiliency needs to/can be developed over time, are you making time to develop yours?**
- Are **you making time** for "mindfulness" and rest?
- There is always something to be grateful for, are you on the lookout for it?

"Our greatest glory is not in never failing, but in rising every time we fail."

–Confucius

... think about it.

Chapter 15

Situational Thinking
... for Better Outcomes!

Life teaches you a new lesson every day, are you attentive enough
to see it and humble enough to learn from it?

–Anonymous

As we wrap up our journey through *Better Outcomes*, I first want to say *thank you* for deciding to spend your valuable time reading this book. I hope it was a good choice and brings you at least a few better outcomes.

The power of Thought

Now, before we end, I wanted to share one final thought with you that I have maintained throughout my career. One that I continually reinforce with myself and others: **Thinking is underrated.** Applying thought, sometimes deep, sometimes shallow, to each situation I have found myself in over the years has helped me immensely. Although this may sound simple, it's the action of stopping yourself from acting first and thinking later that has caused many an issue in your personal and professional life. While being action-oriented is a valuable trait to have, and moving forward with some type of action is better than just standing still for too long, it is action without thought that many times works against getting to better outcomes. Don't fool yourself into thinking that applying thought to a situation will slow that situation down. On the contrary, most of the time, applying some quick thought to a situation will prevent you from having to clean a mess up and thus expedites the end result. It is the oil that enables creativity and innovation. It is the fuel for your future if you look at it that way.

As we finish our journey through this book, I hope you have gained valuable insight into some of the "thinking" you can apply in your own situations. Why do I bring up situations here? That's because everyone is different, and even though we may all be human beings and have similar DNA and characteristics, we have all come from different paths in life. That leads us to today's moment in time where we are all in different situations.

Situational Thinking

Situational thinking is your ability to look at the situation you currently find yourself in, whether it be in a current life situation honed by years of traveling down a certain path or one that just happened upon you a minute ago. Applying situational thinking means having the ability to objectively look at where you are, ask yourself, "why am I here?" or "how did this happen?" and then deciding what to do about it. It is the culmination of applying all your past learnings and life situations to decide something right now about the current situation you are in.

Understanding this simple concept is the completion of this book. If you have noticed, at the end of every chapter, I wrap up with what you can do *to achieve Better Outcomes,* and at the end of that, I added the statement, *"think about it."* The reason for my ending with that is to emphasize that thought is one of the most powerful tools we have as human beings, and the power of thought is sometimes overlooked because of our society's desire for action. Like I said, being action-oriented is a very good thing, but the most valuable action is one that is supported by rational thinking honed by knowledge, experience, and data. It is in the quick and accurate application of these three things where the best decisions come from, and because of the advances in data and analytics, this can

270

happen faster than ever before. Let's look at what I mean by this by applying this thinking to the parts of the book we just went through.

In Part I of this book, we discussed **the power of you**. We started off by asking you to think about where you are today, why you are here, and how you got here. We talked about the power of having an accurate self-assessment of yourself (ASA) and the importance of knowing your own personal 3Cs of characteristics, capabilities, and commitment. Think about the power you now have by knowing these things about yourself and how knowing them will help you make better decisions for the situations you find yourself in going forward.

In Part II of this book, we looked at **the power of being operationally excellent** in all that you do. We discussed taking the time to think about being both effective and efficient in your outcomes and why it was essential to be doing the "right things right" at all times. We followed that up by looking at why wait time is such an efficiency disabler, the importance of being faster-better-cheaper for your customers on an ongoing basis, and why maintaining your innovation is so important. Then we finished up with why you need both management and leadership to be a complete leader for yourself and others.

In Part III of this book, we took some time to think deeply about the individual **characteristics of good leaders** as defined by many and then talked about how nothing is more important than personal leadership of the people you have the honor of leading and getting them what they need to be successful. We then talked about your thinking around change management, how that affects everyone's thinking around a change, and how important it is to introduce and manage the communications around change.

In Part IV, we finished up with the concept of continuous learning, the importance of balance and equilibrium in all that you do, and how having resiliency can help you get through those stressful periods.

So, as you can see, the power of thinking, the power of using the knowledge, experience, and learning you have gained through the years to handle every situation you are in, that's using situational thinking. No matter what, your knowledge is gained in many ways (school, experience, continuous learning, et cetera), and the application of that knowledge is the key to your better outcomes. It is not about how many years you have been on this earth; it really is how much learning went on during those years that are important. It's not how many degrees or certificates you have, it's whether you learned anything during that training that you remember and can apply. It's about whether you have an *accurate self-assessment* (ASA) and *accurate operational assessment* (AOA), and an *accurate leadership assessment* (ALA), which are all about knowing yourself, knowing where you currently are, and knowing whether you have the capabilities and tools to lead and change those.

Remember, do you have twenty years of experience and learning, or one year of experience and learning twenty times? It's up to you to learn more, increase your capabilities, and control that, and thus it's up to you to deliver your *Better Outcomes*!

Thank you for spending the time on this journey with me, and good luck on your quest to achieve *Better OUTCOMES* for yourself, your business, and your career… *remember,* **it all starts, and ends, with you!**

The pages of yesterday cannot be revised, but the pages of tomorrow are blank, and you hold the pen,

… <u>what story are you going to write?</u>

Acknowledgements

To those that made me, shaped me, taught me, guided me, and frankly had to put up with me over the years, whether you knew it or not, you all played a part in helping me make this book possible, I want to say **thank you!**

To my family, to my wife and lifelong partner Barbara, thank you for coming into my life when we were just kids and making it what it is today. You are my guiding conscious, my eternal light, my buddy, my coffee mate, and have made the journey so far more rewarding and fun than I could have ever possibly imagined. Thanks for putting up with me all these years, and I can't wait for more! To Vanessa, Christopher, and Courtney, you are in my thoughts every hour of every day. You are my guiding lights, and sometimes guiding clubs, that keep me honest and up to date in today's world. I learn from you daily, and I am so proud of the adults you have become, the life's you have made, and your focus on making the world a better place for everyone always. To Lucy, I have been a Poppy ever since you came into the world and named me that, and it was, and still is, one of the happiest days of my life. I love you to the moon and back and look forward to more Lago's ice cream cones together… now go crush more of those swimming times!

To my mom, dad, and brother Tom, thank you for bringing me into this world, providing a loving and fun environment to grow up in, for moving to Jackson Heights where I met Barbara. Also, for teaching me to constantly push to be my best, with morals and integrity, and to always keep a helping hand and eye out for the underdog.

To my friends from the old neighborhood, you are too many to name, but like I said in the beginning, whether you know it or not, you all had a part in making this book possible. From playing off-the-ledge in the school yard, to hockey and football in the 78th street park, to hanging out in Budd's in our later years, I wouldn't trade any of it for all the gold in the world; it was priceless!

To my fellow Marines (Pat and Sue, Norm, Terry, Pinky, Donald, and Parris Island, where I learned how much more I could do once I overcame my fears) just to name a few of you. It was in working and accomplishing things with all of you in my early years where I learned that the sooner you stop wasting time and energy talking about why things can't be done, the sooner you can get onto using that wasted energy to get them done!

To my work mentors and leaders, I want to send out a big thanks, especially to Stuart McGuigan whom I had the honor and pleasure of working with for over sixteen years. Together we made an awesome team! Also, to Joe Gill, Bonnie Barit, and Tom Minchello at Hewlett-Packard and Alex Gorsky, Sandi Peterson, Joaquin Duato, Kathy Wengel, Meredith Stevens, Jim Swanson, and the rest of the senior executive team while I was at Johnson & Johnson, thank you for being such great HP Way and Credo-based leaders!

To my past teams and teammates, of which there are too many to name, I say thank you for all your leadership and determination you showed as we accomplished so much in what seems like such a short time. I love and honor you all. And I would be remiss if I didn't thank the final, and in many cases the best, senior leadership team I had the honor to lead in my 30+ year career. Thank you, Arun, Elinor, Guido, Holly, Maryanna, Massimo, Mike R., Mike W., Nigel, Pinki, Sasha, Stephanie, Steve, and Zikar for being such a great and fun team, making it easy for me to bring my best every day. And I want to individually thank my personal savior and executive assistant extraordinaire, Vicki Miller-Leonard. Our time together was too short, but I thank God every day for putting us together. Wishing you and Kenny much happiness and love as you journey down your current and future path together.

To my editor, George Verongos, thanks so much for introducing me to the world of book writing and publishing and for guiding me along the way. Without your guidance and numerous iterations of our manuscript, we would have never gotten where we ended it. Write on my friend!

Lastly, to my friends, especially the Warwick North and South crew, you know who you are. Your influence, and long conversations over a few too many drinks, cigars, and card games, is what made much of this journey worthwhile and provided much of the material for this book, thank you all from the bottom of my heart, and looking forward to more good conversations in the years to come.

Regards and thank you all!

Steve

Notes • References • Credits

Chapter 1

1. Warren Buffett, *Inc. Magazine* (Aug. 27, 2022)
2. Clifton Strength Assessment
3. Myers-Briggs Type Indicator (MBTI)
4. Korn Ferry Global Personality Inventory

Chapter 2

1. *Competitive Advantage: Creating and Sustaining Superior Performance.* Michael Porter, Free Press, 1998, Second Edition. ISBN 0684841460
2. *Good Strategy / Bad Strategy: The Difference and Why it Matters*; Richard P. Remult, Crown Publishing, 2011, ISBN 978-0-307-88623-1

Chapter 3

1. *Good to Great: Why Some Companies Make the Leap... And Others Don't.* J. Collins, Harper Collins; 2001, ISBN 0-06-662099-6
2. *Execution: The Discipline of Getting Things Done.* L. Bossidy, R. Charan, Crown Business, 2002, ISBN 0-609-61057-0
3. *The Effortless Experience: Conquering the New Battleground for Customer Loyalty.* M. Dixon, N. Toman, R. Delisi, Penguin Publishing, CEB, 2013

Chapter 4

1. *Reengineering the Corporation: A Manifesto for Business Revolution.* M. Hammer and J. Champy, Harper Business, 1993, ISBN0-88730-640-3

Chapter 5

1. *The Toyota Way: 14 Management Principles from the World's Greatest Manufacturer.* Jeffrey Liker, McGraw Hill, 2004, ISBN 0-07-139231-9
2. *Built to Last: Successful Habits of Visionary Companies.* J. Collins and J. Porras, Harper Business, 1994, ISBN 0-88730-671-3

Chapter 6

1. *Competing on Analytics: The New Science of Winning.* Tom Davenport, Harvard Business Review, 2007, ISBN 1422103323
2. Balanced Scorecard Norton and Kaplan

Chapter 7

1. *Head, Heart & Guts: How the World's Best Companies Develop Complete Leaders.* D. Dotlich, P. Cairo, S. Rhinesmith, Jossey-Bass, 2006, ISBN 0-7879-6479-4
2. *Unthink: Rediscover Your Creative Genius.* Erik Wahl, Crown Books 2013, ISBN 978-0-7704-3400-7

Chapter 8

1. *Execution: The Discipline of Getting Things Done.* L. Bossidy, R. Charan, Crown Business, 2002, ISBN 0-609-61057-0

Chapter 9

1. *The Project Management Gene.* David Wile, Amazon Publishing, 2021, ISBN 9798754555280
2. *Project to Product.* Mik Kersten, 2018, ISBN 978-1-942-78839-3

Chapter 10

1. *The Ride of a Lifetime...* B. Iger, Random House, 2019, ISBN 978-0-399-59209-6

2. *The 7 Habits of Highly Effective People.* S. Covey Simon & Schuster, 1990, ISBN 0-671-66398-4

3. *The Leadership Challenge.* Kouze & Posner, Jossey-Bass, 2012, ISBN 978-0-470-65172-8

4. *Head, Heart & Guts: How the World's Best Companies Develop Complete Leaders.* D. Dotlich, P. Cairo, S. Rhinesmith, Jossey-Bass, 2006, ISBN 0-7879-6479-4

Chapter 11

1. *On Becoming a Leader.* Warren Bennis, 2009, Basic Books, ISBN-13: 978-0465014088

2. *The One Minute Manager.* K. Blanchard and S. Johnson, 2003, Harper Collins, ISBN 978-0-688-01429-2

3. *Zapp! The Lightning of Empowerment: How to Improve Quality, Productivity, and Employee Satisfaction.* William C. Byham, Ballantine Books, 1997, ISBN-10: 0449002829

4. *Everyone's a Coach: You Can Inspire Anyone to be a Winner.* Don Shula and K. Banchard, Harper Business, 1995, ISBN 0-310-50120-2

5. *Team of Teams: New Rules of Engagement for a Complex World.* Gen. Stanley McChrystal, Portfolio, 2015, ISBN 978-1591847489

6. *The Ideal Team Player: How to Recognize and Cultivate the Three Essential Virtues.* P. Lecioni, Jossey-Bass, 2016, ISBN 978-1-119-20959-1

7. *Tribal Leadership: Leveraging Natural Groups to Build a Thriving Organization.* D. Logan, J. King, H. Fischer-Wright, Harper-Collins, 2008, ISBN978-0-06-125130-6

8. *The Ideal Team Player: How to Recognize and Cultivate the Three Essential Virtues.* P. Lecioni, Jossey-Bass, 2016, ISBN 978-1-119-20959-1

Chapter 12

1. *Leading Change.* John Kotter, 1996, ISBN 0-87584-747-1
2. *Stop Using the Excuse "Organizational Change is Hard."* Nick Tasler, Harvard Business Review, July 19, 2017

Chapter 13

1. Learning retention research by transaction company Otter.ai in partnership with the University of North Carolina.
2. *The Fifth Discipline: The Art & Practice of the Learning Organization.* P. Senge, Doubleday, 2006, ISBN 978-0-385-51725-6
3. *"Where companies go wrong with learning and development,"* Steve Glaveski, 10/02/2019, HBR

About the Author

Steve Wrenn is a transformational business and technology leader with thirty-five-plus years of experience-building and leading high-performing teams and operations. His leadership and experience spans across the globe and encompass roles as varied as being a US Marine Corps Officer, a research engineer at MIT, part of starting and selling a technology company, growing multiple companies' international footprints, leading more than twenty acquisitions / divestitures, and being a senior executive at some of the world's most recognizable companies such as Hewlett-Packard, Liberty Mutual Insurance, CVS, and Johnson & Johnson (J&J)

At J&J from 2013 to 2022, Steve served as SVP and Chief Information Officer (CIO) for J&J's $65B global supply chain. Working closely with the executive leadership team, he was responsible for accelerating the pace of digital innovation across planning, manufacturing, quality, logistics and customer service; delivering key business improvement and growth programs for patients, providers, and consumers; and driving overall digital technology effectiveness and efficiency. Prior to joining J&J, Steve held key leadership positions at CVS, Liberty Mutual Insurance, Cisco Systems, Hewlett-Packard, MIT Lincoln Laboratories and as an NCO and then commissioned officer in the United States Marine Corps.

Steve earned MBA at the University of New Hampshire and has a BS in Engineering Technology from the University of Massachusetts. He is a member of the Industry Advisory Board (IAB) at Rensselaer Polytechnic Institute (RPI) - Lally School of Management, and a member of the College Advisory Board at UNH College of Engineering (CEPS). He is a husband, a proud father, and an even prouder grandfather and currently lives with his wife Barbara in Portsmouth, NH.

Made in United States
Orlando, FL
23 January 2024

42842420R00163